DREAM GARDENS

LEONIE CORNELIUS

MERCIER PRESS

Irish Publisher – Irish Story

CONTENTS

INTRODUCTION

About a year ago I started preparing a course on how to create a garden design from scratch. I had been creating gardens for private and commercial clients on a regular basis, yet actually trying to put my design process down on paper – never mind teaching others – felt a little daunting. Where does one even start?

I had studied both interior architecture and garden design for eight years and my business had been running for five years. I had presented numerous television shows, designed and created three award-winning show gardens at Bloom in the Park in Dublin and Chelsea in Bloom in London. Yet this course was making me nervous! After much stress and cursing – 'I'll never get this done, why did I even take this on?' – I finally completed an outline of my design process.

After running the course and seeing the positive reactions of the participants, I realised that I wanted to share the ideas that I had developed with a wider audience in the form of a book. One reason for this is that great garden design is often considered exclusive. However, I believe that design should be an open discus-sion, something that every homeowner, renter and balcony lover should be able to enjoy. In modern times collaboration and sharing have become important aspects within the general field of garden design, and I feel that if you share your ideas and design process with others so much more comes back to you.

This book aims to give you the skills and inspiration to take on your own garden space, but it is also an invitation to dream a little. Don't limit yourself before you have to. Think big and envisage your dream space and then start on the practical elements. The book also aims to give you a way of opening up your mind to good design and provide you with the tools to create a well-thought-out, well-designed space.

The pages in this volume should empower you to take on your own project, because, after all, you are the one that will be living in your dream space forever.

Happy designing!

Leonie

WHAT YOU NEED TO START YOUR DREAM GARDEN

To start on the process of creating your own dream garden I would first recommend getting a small list of handy items. The one thing that I cannot do without as I'm designing is a small notebook with unlined pages. Wherever I go I always end up collecting notebooks in all shapes and sizes. These are invaluable for jotting down ideas, making sketches and as a collection point for pictures from magazines. Get yourself a pretty one which you will enjoy using.

You will also need some A3 paper. I would recommend using layout paper, as this thin paper is great for rough sketches. Paper, pencils, erasers and sharpeners will also come in handy, and for the 'What Have You Got?' chapter it would be good to have a scale rule, which is a ruler with different scales on it that is often used in building, so that you can draw your site to scale.

REMEMBER: don't be daunted if you can't draw well. This is not an art competition, it's simply a means of exploring your ideas and dreaming up your own beautiful garden space.

YOUR DREAMS | an emotional way of dreaming up a concept

Long before we embark on the actual design of your garden on paper, and before we start looking at the practicalities of your site and design, I want you to consider this – what is your garden dream?

Design choices, practicalities and functions are all important factors in the design process, but the vital first step is figuring out what you want your dream garden to be. At this stage, the founding idea behind your dream garden should be more of an emotion than a description, i.e. how you want the garden to make you feel when you walk into it. Think about it: have you ever walked into a garden and just sighed with the sheer beauty of it? This is not accidental. Well-designed spaces follow the rules of design, but they also have that certain something that makes them more than just a lovely space. They tend to offer an emotional connection.

REMEMBER that this is your garden and your chance to create your very own perfect space. There's one major thing that I always say to my clients at this stage: DREAM BIG.

DREAM BIG

There are no limits at this stage of the design process. There is no budget, no restrictions, not even a site. All that comes later. This stage is about opening your mind and allowing yourself to dream up your most amazing, most inspiring and personally perfect garden space.

DREAM GARDEN DIAGRAMS

Here is a little exercise to get your creative juices flowing: close your eyes and try to think of a garden – public or private – where you felt most at ease and happy. It can be anywhere and anything, from Versailles to a spectacular show garden, or even your granny's back garden

What was it about this garden that appealed to you? Was it the masterfully combined planting? Was it the vibrancy of the chosen colours? Maybe it was the fun approach in accessories or the symmetries of the 'hard landscaping', i.e. the construction materials such as stone, timber, concrete, tarmac or metals that improved the design of the garden. Perhaps it was the dramatic architecture of the structures that stayed with you. Whatever aspect of the garden appealed to you the most is the thing that you want to try to recapture in this exercise.

Now that you have these appealing features in mind, let's do what I call a dream diagram or a brainstorm diagram. This diagram is a depiction of what you imagine your space feeling like. It aims to open up your mind and stop you thinking about all the practical elements for a little while.

To start your diagram, write down the name of the place that inspires you in the middle of a blank page in your notebook – e.g. the Alhambra Gardens – and draw a bubble around the name. Then, above the bubble, I want you to list the appealing characteristics of the place. Underneath the bubble write the moods it evokes for you.

Now let's look at your diagram with its list of characteristics and moods. What elements of this are important to you in your own life, home and garden? Do you crave more symmetry or harmony? Perhaps you want to introduce more fun and wildness into your life and garden? Do you want more tranquillity and privacy?

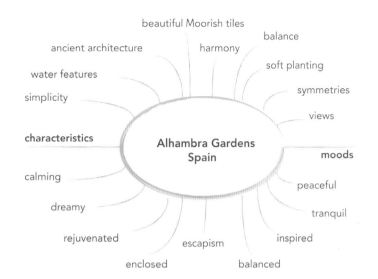

beautiful Moorish tiles

ancient architecture

harmony

balance

water features

soft planting

simplicity

symmetries

views

characteristics

Alhambra Gardens Spain

moods

calming

peaceful

dreamy

tranquil

rejuvenated

escapism

inspired

enclosed

balanced

Identifying your preferred moods is key to designing your space, as this will allow you to build everything in the design around your real mood needs and desires. Following these emotions will ensure that throughout the design process the garden will be totally personalised around you and your dreams. So make sure to keep a note of your preferred moods in your notebook. You will need to keep them in mind as the design process continues.

EXPLORING YOUR LIFESTYLE | your day in the garden

WHO ARE YOU?

After looking at your dreams you must now consider who you are on a practical, everyday level. Bringing this and your dream together will make your design intensely personal, as well as ensuring that it functions well for you.

Ask yourself these questions in order to capture an accurate picture of who you are: What do you like? How do you live now and how would you like to live? What is your current garden style? How does your home feel and look and how do you live your everyday life? Do you have children or pets? Are you single? Do you travel a lot? What does your everyday life in the garden look like? What are your hobbies? For instance, do you read, write, play sports or garden? The answers to these questions will show who you are from a practical and lifestyle perspective.

'how do you live now and how would you like to live?'

Explore your current lifestyle and your current relationship with your garden. Look for what makes you happiest in the day. Is it when you get the chance to read your book on a rickety old bench at the back of the garden in the evening after a long day at work? Or is it long, lazy summer lunches with friends and family on the patio? Make notes of your happy moments in the garden as you go along. Every idea, every thought matters. Get your children and/or partner to do the same.

FUNCTION

Now that you have yourself and your current life-style in mind, write down what it is that you want from your garden. The idea here is to think about the function you would like this garden to fulfil. For example, do you want your garden to become a fun family space? Does the idea of an entertainment space appeal to you? Might you prefer a space that's just for you? Do you want to grow vegetables and fruit? Do you want a space to clear your head? All this matters, as it will inform your approach to the garden.

Your dreams will probably already be a hint as to what you want the garden to do for you. Have a look at the mood words from your dream diagram and see how they line up with what you want from your garden. The function of the garden is to bring that feeling to life. For example, if your dream is to have a space that feels calm, balancing and relaxing, then the design elements and materials must be balanced, planting design and materials calming in character, and there must be space for relaxation.

Great design follows a careful consideration of function. No design is more annoying to live with than the one that just doesn't work. The best-designed garden scheme can become irritating, for example, if circulation does not work and it's hard to move around the space. The prettiest garden may never be used if it does not perform the function that the client desires. Moreover, your garden space may have to perform multiple roles. Broadly speaking, however, we need to enjoy them on a daily basis. Therefore, it is important that we design the garden around what our daily lives entail.

I like to base my list of functions around people's days at home. A list such as the hypothetical one that follows is amazingly helpful. It is a simple overview of what you (and your family) might do in the garden and some of the issues that need to be taken into account when coming up with a design:

- When it is dry I hang out my washing (boring, I know, but functional).

- In warmer weather, when the kids are in school, I pull out my lounger and read a book.

- When the kids are at home and the sun is out they go straight to the hammock between the trees and the trampoline.

- The dog runs riot around the garden.

- I like to sit and admire the plants.

- I do some yoga on the patio, but the neighbours can look straight onto my yoga spot.

- When it rains I have to go inside, as there is no rain cover.

- In the summer I go away for three weeks on holidays.

- I like to entertain.

- The largest amount of people in the garden at one time would be about eight to ten.

- The view to the south from the garden is lovely.

- I need storage for garden equipment.

Once you have completed this list in your note-book, your garden's functional requirements will be clear to you. Again, it is useful to write these requirements down in list form. Here is an example:

What my garden needs:

Washing line

Children's play area

Area for dog

Space to do yoga with privacy screening

Relaxation area with rain cover

Patio entertainment area large enough for up to ten people

Relatively low maintenance plants that can be left during holidays

Improve view from inside to the south of the garden

A shed for storage of garden equipment

Once you have done this, you will have a list of all the functions that your garden needs to fulfil. This is the key to making the garden feel like it's yours. Addressing all these functions in the design will give you a great garden that is designed entirely around your personal needs.

It takes more than addressing functions to make a garden feel truly special, however. To do this you need to ask yourself – what is your style?

FINDING YOUR STYLE | what's yours?

WHAT MAKES A STYLE?

Most people know instinctively what they like and don't like. Even when clients say to me 'design whatever you like', I know that if I don't study their style carefully there's no way the client will be happy with the design.

Style is incredibly personal, you see. When it comes to clothing, for example, we are drawn to certain fabric, colours and styles. This is something that evolves over many years of learning what we like; making personal associations to things like colour and feel, and our cultural associations with different styles. For example, what style means in Europe would differ from what it means in China, Russia or South America, as style generally has its roots in the country's climate, culture and history.

Seen from an anthropological viewpoint, style can be traced back to early humans and their need to distinguish between different tribes. This basic human desire to differentiate ourselves is still one that we see in the design choices humans make today. If you look at the clothing choices we make or the accessories or furnishings we surround ourselves with, you will see that they still hint at a sort of tribal mentality. Examples of this can be anything from modern-day tribes such as hipsters and Goths, to more task-orientated tribes like surfers, skate-boarders and musicians. The same goes for interior style.

From minimalist Scandinavian style to vintage cottage living, these styles have strong connections with a way of life and offer many climatic, cultural and historical inspirations from which to draw.

Over our lifetime we develop our own styles, based on the people that surround us (our tribe), our collective histories and the climate we live in, as well as other inspirations from around the globe. We mentally collect visuals of ideas, fabrics and styles – often without even realising – and create style palettes in our own heads that we can tap into at will. We know that we like the blue couch – we are not sure why – but just know instinctively that it's the one we would choose.

When it comes to garden design you may not think you are as knowledgeable – particularly about the various styles – but once we start looking at the different garden styles you will no doubt surprise yourself by recognising many of them.

WHAT ABOUT GARDEN TRENDS?

Trends often follow what the big names in garden design are doing at the Royal Horticultural Society (RHS) shows in the UK, such as the Chelsea Flower Show, Hampton Court Flower Show or Tatton Park, or here in Ireland at Bloom in the Park. These show garden festivals are where the top garden designers display their designs to the public once a year, and are a great place to study different styles.

Often these gardens are more than just a visually appealing approach to gardening. They often display environmentally conscious solutions to planting and gardening in general. The gardens by James Basson at the Chelsea Flower Show are one such example – one of his show gardens created a sustainable solution to planting in the Provence area of France by choosing only plants that would thrive in the dry soil of the area, thus cutting out the need for extra irrigation.

Trends within show gardens can also develop around social causes. From the Syrian refugee crisis being referenced at Bloom in the Park, and modern slavery at the Chelsea Flower Show, these gardens can be valuable tools in the fight to highlight the need for support, care and advocacy in the modern world. Gardens can also bring an awareness of environmental problems to the public, such as highlighting the plastic pollution in the sea. The ideas from gardens created by talented designers at these shows often trickle down to designers everywhere, and bold new approaches can have a strong impact on how designers from all over tackle their projects.

Many clever designers will also look beyond the bubble of garden shows and seek out trends happening in other design fields, such as architecture, furniture or fashion. I think this is a very strong way of ensuring that garden designs stay fresh, vibrant and current.

Though not a strict follower of trends, I do love how a new trend in a material or a colour can work its way into a garden in a subtle way and give it a fresh new face. The trend for copper in interior design, for example, found its way into my garden at Bloom in the Park 2013, where I used it in fencing and metal detailing on the custom-designed chair. For those who have a keen interest in current fashions, colour palettes and materials in your garden accessories or planting additions can often cleverly reference a trend. These have the added benefit that they can be gently adjusted to change over time.

'seek out trends happening in other design fields, such as architecture, furniture or fashion'

I feel that all genres of design – whether architecture, fashion, film, food or others – are connected in a way in which they can all inform each other. Other genres of art and design are an endless source of inspiration and this idea of 'cross-pollination' can be a very successful tool in the design process. For example, the colours of a dress by a fashion designer may work its way into the palette of a planting combination, or the texture of ceramics into the feel of a wall finish. In this way we can take inspiration from art and design and create our own new and personalised garden.

STYLES

When it comes to actual garden styles there are many ways of exploring them, and in this section I have broken these down into the main categories. Sometimes this is done by the country of origin and other times it is done by a feeling, such as romantic. I will try to include examples from both of these categories, as they do tend to cover slightly different angles.

The definition of style is 'a distinctive appearance, typically determined by the principles according to which something is designed'. Style becomes apparent within gardens when all parts of a garden are in harmony with each other and every aspect of the design follows one approach. For example, if the style is 'sleek contemporary', then every material, colour and accessory must mirror this. In order to achieve this, materials will most likely be smooth and modern in finish – such as concrete or smooth stone – accessories will be minimalist in design rather than fussy, and colours are likely to be understated and chosen from a limited palette.

'every material within the design should reference that style'

Similarly, with an ethnic style every material within the design should reference that style. It is imperative that every boundary, colour, accessory and plant makes sense within the context of that style. Mexican-style gardens, for example, will most likely feature strong structural planting that reference the native, desert-style planting and the colours could echo the warm, earthy tones of terracotta with, perhaps, bold splashes of pinks.

Consider the design to the left. This garden by Alan Rudden for Santa Rita Estates has been designed with the landscape of Chile in mind. Every detail has been carefully chosen to reflect the style of the locality, from the earthy and natural colours of the structural elements, to the planting which echoes the indigenous Chilean landscape, such as soft grasses, strong structural plants and the solidity of the thick-stemmed olive trees. This garden has succeeded in perfectly summing up the Chilean landscape in a garden here in Ireland.

If done carefully and organically, using styles from other cultures or climate zones can be incredibly exciting and distinctive. However, you have to be very careful that the garden still has a connection to its actual locale, the structures around it and the people living beside it. If you lose that, the garden can become a caricature of a style.

When it comes to some other styles, the approach may be about more than a cultural or emotional influence. Rather it could be an answer to a functional need, such as requiring a self-sufficient garden or a family-style garden. These are based around require-

'using styles from other cultures or climate zones can be incredibly exciting and distinctive'

ments that override a national style. Of course, there is nothing to say that you can't pick and choose your style from both and perhaps even attempt to create special areas for both. For example, if you are drawn to a beautiful, formal French style but have a big family that needs everything from trampolines to swing sets, then – providing you have enough space – you could create separate areas. This way all your needs can be met and your favourite style still has a chance to shine. Be careful, however, as it can get messy and the aim is to try to be subtle.

CONTEMPORARY STYLE | Our Gardens Now

Most gardens designed now have some form of contemporary approach, i.e. 'of the now'. It is for this reason that trends tend to play a large role in this style. This means that we should be thinking about what is currently happening in the various worlds of design and how we can incorporate these ideas into the design. We can do this in a number of ways, such as by considering what materials are being used in interior design, or by looking at what is happening in the world of fashion, art and music. These can all be rich sources of inspiration for making a garden feel contemporary.

Another trend-based aspect to consider in designing contemporary-style gardens is how we approach the environmental challenges of our current times. For example, many contemporary-style gardens create clever solutions to rainwater collection, shade solutions or other vital elements in order to create a sustainable garden. For instance, cleverly adapted planting for dry conditions may be a solution to rainwater shortages.

We can approach this sustainability issue in our own gardens by considering our needs and what will make the garden more self-sufficient in the future. If we think about simple things at the start of the design process, such as making our own compost or methods of collecting rainwater, then it can become an integral part of the design rather than being tagged on at a later stage.

The contemporary style also takes into consideration how, in modern times, we have seen a massive change in how much time we spend outdoors. In response to this, the contemporary style tends to blur the distinction between the inside and outside of the house. I find spaces that bring the inside and the outside together exciting to be in, and these outdoor 'rooms' really challenge our traditional perception of 'garden' and 'interior'.

This style is a very exciting one as it can be easily combined with other styles, making it incredibly versatile.

Design elements:

Clean, sleek design forms; contemporary structures and materials; sustainable solutions for climatic challenges; areas for garden living, such as outdoor kitchens or entertainment spaces.

GARDENS OF THE WORLD | Mirrors of Culture and History

Persian-style Gardens

The Persian-style garden is a fitting place to start when we talk about different cultural garden styles. When I was studying garden design in college I loved learning that the common Iranian word for 'enclosed space' was *pari-daiza* – a word later adopted by Christians to describe the Garden of Eden. The word itself translates as 'paradise'. You see, the idea of the Persian garden was to create a paradise on earth for the user.

Fascinatingly, some historians argue that the origin of gardens overall can be traced back to Persian gardens. These well-thought-out spaces of beauty were places for relaxing, entertaining and praying. Sophisticated design elements that dealt with sunlight, water and the blending of inside with outside spaces were found in these gardens, features that are still the basis of our practices today and inform many of our modern design choices.

Many Persian gardens, whether private or public, were enclosed by a wall to help create that feeling of paradise on earth. The space would have often been cooled by sophisticated water elements, including rills, fountains and underwater irrigation channels called 'qanats'. Sunlight played a major role in the overall architecture of structures, being channelled to highlight shapes and textures in the spaces.

One of my all-time favourite places to visit is the Alhambra in Granada. This palace and the surrounding gardens on the Andalusian coast are a breathtaking example of the principles of Persian-style garden design. It is a perfect example of how spaces inside were connected to the outside via arches and roofed walkways. Even the enclosed courtyard with the water rill feels semi-enclosed, almost like a room outside.

Design elements:

Symmetrical designs; enclosed walls; sophisticated water features; clever shade and light solutions; roofed walkways; arches.

Far Eastern-style Gardens

Far Eastern garden design has strong elements of spirituality attached to it. Both Chinese and Japanese gardens are based strongly around balance and scale and these gardens often represent wider landscapes recreated in miniature form – for example, a simple mounding of soil in landscaping and perfectly pruned shrubs can represent distant hills and mountains, and miniature trees such as Japanese maples or bonsai forms can represent their larger versions.

Japanese garden design evolved from the much earlier, sacred Chinese gardens and there are definite design elements that carry across both styles. The earliest Chinese gardens, dating back to the Shang Dynasty (1600–1046 BC), would have been large parks where the nobility hunted game. These spaces were also the first to treat the garden as a miniature representation of a wider landscape and a classical Chinese garden aimed to create a series of perfectly arranged views, each framed to be admired from many angles. The idea of never seeing the whole garden in one view was integral to this approach and aimed to lead the visitor around the space by glimpses of beautiful natural compositions.

When looking at Far Eastern gardens we are often invited to observe and not necessarily touch – think, for example, of the raked Zen gravel gardens that are painstakingly prepared and yet destined never to be walked upon. The thought process behind this – and most traditional Far Eastern gardens – is to create an area of tranquillity and thus calm the mind.

Regular features in the Far Eastern-style garden include mounding shrubs (one that takes on a mounded shape when grown), such as azaleas and rhododendron, as well as colourful autumn acers and bamboo for movement. Adopting elements of this style in your garden can be a great way of creating space and calm, and the elegant simplicity of this style of planting appeals to many modern garden lovers.

The underlying design processes of a Far Eastern-style garden are incredibly sophisticated and can be very hard to get right unless you have in-depth knowledge of Oriental culture, history and religion. The key to getting this style right is to be selective and use few materials. You want to avoid the garden becoming a caricature of the Far Eastern garden, so keep it simple.

A bonus for this style of garden is that many of the plants often chosen for Far Eastern gardens mostly do very well in north-western Europe due to the similar climate. Japanese maples, for example, do very well here and provide stunning autumnal foliage. Mosses, ferns, bamboos and trees such as the flowering cherry and ilex varieties also live happily in our gardens.

Design elements:

Miniature landscapes based on larger settings; paddle stones; raked gravel; dry streams; niwaki (cloud pruned) trees; cloud pruned shrubs; elegantly placed structures; calming colour palettes, dominated by green; pebble and water features; stone lanterns; waterspouts; koi ponds with koi carp.

New World Style

The feeling of the New World-style garden (USA, Australia and more) is rooted in a sense of freedom and wide-open spaces. It seeks to emulate expanses such as the beautiful North American prairie and the landscapes of the Australian outback. This style is fresh and vibrant and tends to include a contemporary approach to design elements.

The most popular feature of New World-style garden design at the moment is the prairie or naturalistic style of garden planting. Mainly this involves a planting approach that has its roots in the North American prairies and it is used in many places worldwide, such as the High Line project in New York by master plantsman Piet Oudolf.

The idea behind this style is far more than simply creating a good planting composition. Here we are attempting to create a composition that will become as self-sustainable as possible. The naturalistic approach to planting is one that aims to create a balanced ecosystem for wildlife and echoes how nature actually grows. I am a big fan of the loose, dreamy planting of the prairie-style garden and it is a wonderful style of planting to choose for wildlife, as it has many important aspects such as bee-friendly plants and plants that self-seed, thus ensuring that seed-heads will be left for the birds and insects to feed on over the winter months.

This style tends to suit people who take a keen interest in living outdoors, which is certainly something that we are placing more importance on in our own lifestyles and garden designs these days.

Design elements:

Outdoor living spaces; loose, prairie-style planting which is allowed to evolve over time; contemporary structures; naturalistic planting; an emphasis on plant ecology and sustainability; wildlife encouraging.

WESTERN-STYLE GARDENS | The Development of a European Garden Style

Medieval-style Gardens

European or Western-style gardens have many faces. Originating in the medieval gardens of monasteries and castles, these gardens placed more emphasis on the aesthetics of a garden than what had come before. Monastery gardens, for example, were often designed around the shape of the cross, representing Christ — a layout that was ideal for contemplation, prayer and meditation. The emphasis placed on creating an overall design for the space also meant that they were very aesthetically pleasing spaces to be in.

These gardens were also laid out in a clever way. Using divisions, for example in planting beds laid out in grid systems, added to the visual appearance of the garden, but it also worked for ease of access. This was particularly useful as these gardens were often used to grow necessary produce for the users, such as herbs used in cooking and some medicinal plants. As a result, the medieval-style garden can be a very good reference point for those interested in creating beautiful gardens with an emphasis on self-sufficiency.

Design elements:

Layout in the shape of a cross; clever division of the garden; a mix of aesthetically pleasing flowers, plant and food crops; calming design features; medicinal planting.

Italian-style Gardens

Created in the fifteenth-century Renaissance period, these gardens were linked to classical architecture and the enjoyment of the garden space. Inspired by descriptions of ancient Roman gardens (which in turn were inspired by the earlier Persian gardens), these were created at wealthy villas, such as those found in Florence and Rome, and were places where the owners could both enjoy the sensual spaces and create breathtaking spectacles in order to showcase their power and wealth.

The main elements of the Italian garden style were inspired by classical ideals of beauty and order. The gardens had strong symmetrical elements with features that were often grandiosely playful and surprising. They included fun water games and elaborate water features with spumes of water and even water organs that played music.

In his *Ten Books on Architecture*, Leon Battista Alberti (1404–1472) set out the rules of design for the Renaissance garden. He wrote that the Italian garden should be lower than the villa, creating a stronger view of the garden from the building. He also argued that spaces should be created within the garden, allowing the user to look back admiringly at the house. He gave many instructions for how the garden should be designed and specified everything, from how to structure trees in planting to creating shaded porticos (classical-style porches) and specifying what type of sculpture was most suitable for this style of garden.

Overall, the formal Italian design was strongly based on symmetry, repetition and formal layouts. Designs of the time were created to delight and impress visitors, as well as being an obvious sign of the wealth and power of the owner. For example, the ruling family of Florence in the sixteenth century, the Medicis, commissioned elaborate and spectacular gardens. Examples of these, such as the beautiful Boboli gardens, can still be admired today. The gardens often included many structural features, such as elaborate columns, porticos and statues that were created by the leading architects, sculptors and artists of the Renaissance. The gardens also often had *giardini segreto* (secret gardens), which could be discovered by the owner or the adventurous visitor.

When broken down, the formal Italian design approach is a great tool for designing in smaller spaces as the strong symmetries, water features and repetitive elements can be easily adapted to suit smaller spaces. These features can be a good starting point for a garden design that is inspired by the formal Italian style.

Design elements:

Strong formal symmetries; avenues of rare trees for shade; the repetition of elements; garden lower than house; water tricks and games; statues and fountains; secret garden areas.

French-style Gardens

Similar to the Italian garden, the French-style garden takes its design cues from strong symmetrical layouts and repetition. The idea of taming nature is a strong element of French design; it strives to create order and structure.

French formal garden style evolved from the Renaissance-era Italian gardens. It was actually King Charles VIII who brought the Italian style of garden to France when he returned from Italy in 1495. The king commissioned a spectacular Italian-style garden at his residence, the Château d'Amboise in the Loire Valley in France.

Interestingly, gardens at this time in Italy and France were still very much separate from the castle or residence and were often contained in a walled enclosure. It was not until 1656 that the first true French-style garden was created. It was in Maincy near Paris, where a talented team came together to create the gardens at Vaux-le-Vicomte. The team consisted of the landscape architect André Le Nôtre, architect Louis Le Vau and the painter-decorator Charles Le Brun. This project, which was commissioned by Nicolas Fouquet – the superintendent of finances to Louis XIV – combined architecture, landscape design and interior design. This blending of different fields of design had been unheard of until that point.

The true highlight of the French garden style is undoubtedly the garden of Versailles in Paris, which was designed by André Le Nôtre between 1661 and 1700.

It is a breathtaking example of formal French garden design. The layout of this garden is rooted in the Italian style, with strong symmetry and geometric shapes, and is simply stunning in its intricacy and detail. Built for the 'Sun King', Louis XIV, these vast gardens span an area of 15,000 hectares and were the largest in Europe at the time. A large circular fountain in the garden represents the king's symbol: the sun. Many gardens in this period had mythological references, and this garden features a sculpture of the Greek sun god Apollo in the middle of the main fountain. The garden was designed to fan out from the central palace and have views that seemed to stretch out forever. The overall idea was to create something spectacular to show the dominance and power of the king and how he ruled over his land, his territories and even nature.

Other notable elements of this garden style that can be found at Versailles include the parterre, which is quintessentially French in style. The parterre is a formally laid out planting bed with clipped structural hedges elaborately designed like filigree and surrounded by gravel paths. Other design elements typical to the French style are allées. These are long symmetrical alleys, often tree-lined, that lead the user through the space. Topiary is also a very strong element of French garden style, a feature whereby trees and shrubs are shaped into quite formal and elaborate ornaments.

Plans for the French-style garden are quite geometric and often fan out in many directions, making this a design style that works wonderfully for larger sites.

These gardens also place a firm emphasis on creating links between the house and the garden, as well as ensuring that one can view the house – or, more commonly, château – from a distance.

Planting in French formal gardens was often quite simple, but perfectly pruned and maintained, signifying the power of man over nature. Elements of the formal French style such as parterres and allées can still be found in many contemporary garden designs today. The designer Dominique Lafourcade, for example, masterfully combines traditional French-style garden elements with a modern approach.

Design elements:

Formal symmetrical layout; a design spanning out from the buildings or on a central axis; elaborate parterres; tree-lined allées; controlled planting and simple colour schemes; bodies of water and fountains; sculptures that often have mythological references; strong views from the house, which is usually the centre of the scheme; a terrace to enjoy the views.

English-style Gardens

Up until the eighteenth century, gardens across Europe were principally French in style with rigid formal lines and an aim to control the wildness of nature. During the eighteenth century, however, a style of garden emerged in England that was considered more informal in approach than its Italian or French predecessors. The English garden, or 'English landscape garden' as it was also known, was conceived around the idea of a return to a more natural style of garden.

This development occurred for a number of reasons. For one thing, it coincided with the Romantic Movement, which was in part an answer to the Industrial Revolution. This movement saw an increased interest in nature, beauty, art, poetry and literature. Romanticism placed a strong emphasis on emotion and individualism rather than conformity or the controlling of nature. Another more practical reason for this development in garden design was the incredibly high maintenance required for the purely formal Italian and French-style gardens.

In essence, this English landscape garden intended to create an idealised version of the natural garden. The earlier English-style gardens, such as those by landscape architect Capability Brown, are examples of this style. This style was totally new for this time, embracing the surrounding nature as part of the immediate garden around the house and thus blurring the line between garden and landscape. Elements of this style included softly undulating grasses and sweeping views to serpentine lakes. Ultimately this style was considered a 'garden-less' form of garden design, one that almost felt like it had not been designed.

Interestingly, the English garden as we know it today takes reference not only from this 'garden-less' approach, but also from an Asian style of garden. Asian gardens at the time had a far more informal approach to garden design compared to the French style. The aim of the Asian garden was to emulate the irregular way in which nature grows and so symmetry and order were intentionally avoided. One lasting influence this Asian inspiration had on the development of the English garden was the looser, more informal flower borders we know today as the 'English border'.

All these different factors went into making the English-style garden that we know today. This is sometimes referred to as the 'English cottage garden'.

These gardens sit as well beside a stately manor as they do beside a cottage by the sea. They feature a mix of clever structural and formal lines, such as low hedging, mixed with looser, seemingly random planting and sweeping flower borders full of interest in height, texture and colour. They also maintain many influences from its evolving past, such as loose shrubberies against woodland backdrops, which reminds us of the English landscape style, while some have gravelled walkways that hint at the Italian and French styles.

This cottage-style garden is a homely version of the more formal English garden and is one of the best styles to use for smaller gardens. It allows for a certain wildness in planting, which makes it easier to maintain. It also mixes both formal elements from the English garden, such as structural box hedging, with more informal characteristics and looser planting as a contrast.

Design elements:

Woodland views; mounded expanses of lawns leading to natural water features; box hedging to neaten edges of beds; strong colour-filled herbaceous planting beds or borders; areas of lawn, rambling climbers; terraces; pruned, ball-and-box-shaped trees and shrubs.

GARDENS BY CLIMATE

Climate zones can also inspire garden styles. Here are some examples.

Tropical Style | Creating a Tropical Haven in your Garden

Creating a tropical-style garden in Ireland may sound a little far-fetched, but with clever plant choices this is actually quite doable. The foundation for creating that tropical feel is a rich texture and plenty of green. Many of our native ferns such as Dryopteris, Polystichum or Asplenium have a distinctly tropical feel, and some hardy evergreen accent plants such as the Fatsia *japonica* can give great structure to garden planting throughout the year. Large-leaved plants such as Acanthus *mollis* are also great additions as the leaves have a wow factor in themselves – the spires of flowers are a bonus. Mix all this with some bold colour blocks and your garden could really have that rainforest feel.

If we break down the tropical garden into its different elements we can consider what makes it look the way it does. One aspect to consider is the habit of a plant. This refers to the characteristic appearance and shape of a plant, as well as the way it grows. Plants in tropical climates are often large-leaved, for example, in order to catch the rain and channel it to the plant's roots – think of banana plants with their huge and elegant leaves. This can be a clue as to what plant shapes will provide you with the feel of a tropical space. Colour is another important factor. Rich deep green hues with dramatic accents will make the garden feel more tropical and lush. Plants such as black bamboos or golden-stemmed varieties are a good starting point for introducing appropriate colour. If you have a very sheltered courtyard then you will get away with using tender plants such as the banana tree, which really gives that tropical feel.

I also love large-leaved plants such as those from the Gunnera family, which can look a lot like the rhubarb in leaf but are far larger. And there is the Dicksonia *antarctica*, the 'tree fern', which looks about as tropical as it gets in our landscape. Lilies, daylilies and Crocosmia are also a wonderful way of introducing some exoticism and rich colour into a tropical-style space. Kniphofias (red-hot pokers) also have that sunny, tropical feel and do well in our climate. Grasses such as the Hakonechloa *macra* can have a really tropical feel to them if combined with the right elements and also fare very well in our climate. You can also cheat a little and include a few tender plants such as the stunning – if delicate – Canna lily in your design and bring them inside when it gets a little colder.

Design elements:

Structured foliage; textured leaves; textured and coloured stems; spires of rich warm colours; hot-looking plants such as Dahlias and Cannas; dramatic architectural shapes.

Desert Style | Taking Inspiration from Dry Climates

Achieving a successful desert style in our climate is a very tricky thing to do. Those of us lucky enough to have glasshouses will find this a lot more doable. In a glasshouse – even an unheated one – cacti and succulents will thrive and, if cleverly combined, you can really create a desert-style space. Succulents (plants that have fat and fleshy leaves in order to store large amounts of water) and cacti are both plants that have adapted to harsh, arid climates. I am a big fan of these tough little plants and love how they grow and evolve over time in a glasshouse. There is nothing more spectacular than seeing a cactus in full flower. The added bonus with these plants is that they require very little maintenance, making them great plants for people who are very busy. They are also a great way to bring some nature into your home as they do very well on windowsills.

If you really love the style and warmth of desert gardens, but don't have a glasshouse, then think about bringing elements of the warmth and sandy feel of the desert into your garden. Rich terracotta, sandy gravel beds and warm tones in planting would be effective in giving a feel of a warmer climate.

Design elements:

Collections of many of one type of plant, such as a large group of Aloe or Echeveria varieties in one planter for impact; terracotta shades of colour; dry gravel and sand beds; succulents in mounds of varying heights; terracotta accents, such as pots and saucers; large loose pebbles for structure.

THE 'NEED' POINT OF VIEW

Garden style can also be looked at from a 'need' point of view. The idea here is to create a garden based around your needs and passions, such as a self-sufficient or a more family-focused garden. For example, if you are a flower collector this need point of view will be a great style around which to base your garden. It is likely that some other styles will also feed into this design but it's a great starting point, as the style will be customised around you.

Self-sufficient gardens

Many people nowadays are returning to growing their own food. Quality and taste is one huge factor in this change, as people have become frustrated with how every in-store product is streamlined to look, taste and feel the same. We are spoiled for choice in supermarkets with mangos from Brazil and apples from China. Many people, however, are beginning to recognise that this way of producing and purchasing food is not sustainable. Farmers' markets have once again become an important place to source local, seasonal produce and many restaurants and top chefs are leading the way by sourcing local meat, fish, fruit and vegetables that are in season.

I think that growing your own food is an incredibly rewarding experience. No matter how much time you have to spend in the garden, there's always some fruit, vegetable or herb that will do well with limited maintenance. Even if it's just a few strawberries on a balcony, the result is very satisfying.

The ideal self-sufficient gardens are the ones that really take on the idea of growing as much produce as possible throughout the year. This is a way of ensuring that the food you eat is fresh and has not been mass-produced or treated with chemicals. The great thing is that if you have a bit of time, it's virtually free.

For smaller urban gardens the idea of becoming totally self-sufficient is, of course, not realistic, but think about what you could produce with a few clever timber planters or containers. Or you could grow things upright in really tight spaces – peas, beans and other climbers, for example, would do great on cramped south-facing balconies. Hanging edible plants in creative containers is also a great way of ensuring you always have something fresh to munch on.

Design elements:

Areas for growing produce such as raised beds, containers or larger planting beds; a good mix of butterfly- and bee-friendly plants for pollination of crops; loose, natural-looking compositions which can be enhanced by adding colourful flowers; potting sheds or areas for storing harvested crops.

Family Garden Style

A well-designed garden will meet the functions required to live well and make a space usable and joyful. When it comes to families, however, these requirements start to take on a whole new meaning. The family garden places plenty of demands on the design process, from how we circulate around the space, to storage for equipment such as lawn mowers, and the practical aspects of placing utility items such as washing lines and compost areas.

Personally I think the key to getting it right is to make sure that every need is met in terms of the user, while also ensuring that the whole family can be together. A well-designed family garden will consider how the family interacts and give them space to use it together, as well as giving each person a certain amount of room to enjoy their individual garden pursuits.

Family gardens should be fun and exciting. One important aspect is the option for children of being outside, getting muddy and exploring different areas. Safety and fun are the two most vital elements of this style when taking children into account.

Design elements:

Areas for the family to eat together; a spot for growing for the kids (I love how proud children are when they pick their own strawberries or take some home-grown carrots out of the ground); fun and playful elements for children, such as swings, games, safe water games, etc.

Flower Arranger's Garden

This style is one I included because I absolutely love the idea of designing a space around the beauty of flowers. The example shown here is designed around all-season flower availability and is home to talented plantswoman Annette Coleman, who has a thriving wildflower florist business. I personally love having fresh flowers in the home and really enjoy how home-grown flower arrangements change through the seasons. Over the past couple of years there has been a resurgence in people growing flowers themselves or to sell on a local scale. This can be seen in the numerous farmers markets around the country, many of which sell Irish grown and wild flowers. This is a wonderful and much-needed trend, as we often take for granted where the cut flowers on our tables come from. Many of the pretty flowers on our tabletops have flown long distances to get to our supermarkets and, more often than we realise, have been grown and picked in places like Africa, where labour is cheap and laws on chemical control are non-existent. What better way to combat this non-sustainable consumer habit than to grow some flowers for picking yourself?

I also think that the process of growing flowers is so much more satisfying than simply buying them in a supermarket or florist. With clever planning the garden can have a selection of blooms from which you can choose all year round. A small polytunnel growing structure or glasshouse ensures that the arranger has a head start early in the season and here the designer grows plants such as dahlias, sweet pea and cornflowers.

In springtime there is a massive range of bulbs that emerge and in summer this garden is a true explosion of colour: sages, lavenders, verbena and hundreds of roses cover the garden, while yarrow plants and spires of foxgloves rise out of the ground under the shade of trees. Massive dahlias make for some very beautiful and long-lasting bouquets and the parasol-shaped Achillea makes a great filler plant. Autumn is a time in the flower arranger's garden where we see rich shades of gold come into their own. Chinese lanterns – Physalis *alkekengi* – and lovely textural twigs are great for making Halloween wreaths. Twigs are also useful for contemporary arrangements for vases. During winter, foliage of shrubs and twigs really come in useful in arrangements. Trees and plant varieties such as those of the Mahonia, Eucalyptus, Skimmia and Sarcococca families are also beautiful in arrangements and are lovely mixed with a few flowers.

This garden has masses of flowers that form stunning vistas and so many special garden rooms, and yet almost all of the flowers work for flower arranging. It is a stunning example of how to combine profession with passion and a great way to surround yourself with beauty at home. The need here is for plenty of flowers for arranging, as well as there always being enough planting in the garden so that it looks beautiful in itself.

Design elements:

Masses of colourful flowers, cleverly arranged; a seasonal approach to planting ensuring that there are always fresh flowers to choose from; clever choices of planting to ensure there is a good balance of textural foliage interest and flowers for arranging; flowers with scent; a good mix of flower shapes, from ball shapes to fluffy seed-heads and spires, ensuring that there are different heights and forms for bouquets.

Entertainment Garden

Many of my clients want a garden that works as a party or entertainment space. This style of garden needs to strike a delicate balance between being a comfortable and calm space to be in, while also being a space in which it's exciting for people to dine and come together. Here, we need to consider the amount of people you are likely to entertain, as this will be important in terms of safety. Night-time lighting and materials will play a major role in this style of garden. Elements such as barbecues or outdoor kitchen spaces will need to be considered, as well as options for rain cover. Pergolas, outdoor summerhouses or gazebos all feature prominently in spaces where people want to entertain.

If you would like this to be an emphasis in your own space, then consider some form of rain cover, such as a pergola with glass, or some form of inside-outside connection. Consider, too, how you want people to feel in the space. Colour and material choices will be based around this. For example, do you want the garden to have a vibrant and fun atmosphere? If you prefer it to be an elegant and calm dining space for parties, then this will need to be shown in your design details. Party gardens are gardens that can really benefit from having a strong style or theme attached to them. For example, if the space is to be a fun and happy space, then why not consider giving the garden a Mexican-style accent? The rich oranges and terracotta would be a great warm and welcoming starting point, and including an ethnic style in the garden will give you some fun things to play around with and ultimately make your choices of everything from colour to materials a lot easier.

Design elements:

Level areas for entertaining and dining such as decking or patios; outdoor dining ideas such as outdoor kitchens or barbecues; lighting for night-time, both for safety and ambience; rain-cover options, such as pergolas or summer-houses; beautiful views to enjoy while entertaining, such as strong planting areas or focal features like sculptures or water features.

So you can see that there are many styles you can take inspiration from for your garden. There is truly something for every taste and mood. In large part, style is derived from you and your likes and needs, as well as the location of the site and the atmosphere you want to create in your space. If you choose carefully, this style will help bring your garden to life.

YOUR NEW CONCEPT | an emotional way of dreaming up a concept

So, now that we have looked at styles, let's get your concept together. A concept is a summary of your idea or plan for your space. It is made up of your preferred moods, your chosen style and your functional requirements.

The reason for creating a concept is that you have a succinct intention of design which you can keep coming back to for inspiration at every stage of the design process. This concept is your design reference and should inform every choice you make, whether it's about colours, materials, shape, forms, planting or accessories.

Here's how to get your dream concept together:

Choose a few of the strongest elements from your dream garden diagram exercise (see page 15). Combine them with the main functions of your potential garden as discussed on pages 20–23. Now add your preferred style of garden.

Here's mine as an example:

1. Dream garden elements: elegant, symmetrical, calming.

2. Main functions: entertainment and relaxation space.

3. Style elements: Persian, naturalistic, wildlife, modern/ contemporary materials.

So my concept for my dream space would be this:

An elegant, symmetrical space that's calm and perfect for relaxation and entertaining. The style should have Persian influences and naturalistic planting that brings in wildlife, with an emphasis on using modern/contemporary materials.

Note that this concept has one thing that sits slightly out from the ancient feel of the Persian-inspired garden: the modern materials. I added these to highlight one of my main tips for designing high-quality gardens – that it is always beneficial to include something in a concept that is slightly surprising and stops the concept from being too expected. The modern materials will challenge us to look beyond the Persian garden as mere replication and to think about how it fits into the contemporary times in which we live. I believe this added element of surprise should be in every concept as it keeps the design vital and exciting.

The key to great design is putting all these elements from the concept together and making them work in harmony with each other. You can see how the concept in this chapter is easy to understand, and so when you go about choosing colours, shapes and materials, your concept will be incredibly helpful in making well-informed and well-thought-out decisions.

Now try to identify your own personal concept.

WHAT MAKES GOOD DESIGN | principles of design explained

Good design is often instinctive. Some people are naturally great at the placing of objects – for example, the arranging of flowers or hanging pictures on the wall. Even if you don't fall into that category of 'instinctively good designers', there are principles that apply to designing everything from pens to cars and gardens that can be learned. Everybody that has ever studied design knows how important these core principles are in getting a design right.

Let's have a look at these now.

'good design is often instinctive'

UNITY AND HARMONY: HOUSE, GARDEN AND SETTING

This principle of good design is about bringing coherence and a concordance into the design process. Your aim is to achieve something similar to the composition of a beautiful piece of music or a masterfully put-together painting. It should all fit together. A unified and harmonious garden makes you simply want to be in the space.

This can be done in various ways. Linking the house (inside and out) to the garden and making them feel like the one space by using materials, details and the user's style is a great way to create unity and harmony. To achieve this, the style of the interior should be referenced in the garden. You can pick up on materials within the house, such as tiles or timber, and repeat these in ways outside.

For example, you could choose a stone tile that has been used inside the house and use the same tile outside in the garden. This is a great way of creating a connection and making a garden feel visually unified with the interior. This becomes especially important if we have strong connections between the inside and outside, such as a large expanse of open glass to the garden.

I love to bring the inside of the house into the garden space and vice versa. Maybe consider bringing plants that echo the garden into your interior space too. This is a powerful way of inviting nature into your home and bringing your living area outside. When this is all linked again to a larger context, such as the countryside beyond or beautiful views, then you have fascinating and harmonious layers of connection that create a sense of place and unify the design over all levels.

You should also consider linking the garden to the existing site and setting. This will give a sense of space and location and feel like a natural extension of the site. Consider how the landscape is shaped beyond the boundary of the garden. Are there ways to reference that in planting shape or colour in the garden? This will have such a strong impact on the feeling of the garden and give it a real sense of space. You can also achieve this using planting that repeats views or colours, or references local settings.

Other things to consider here are the shapes you use in the garden. Much like hanging a collection of artworks, there is a harmonious way to create form in the garden. The best way to achieve harmony here is to have one large shape that dominates as a focal point, such as a circular lawn or a square paved area, and team this with a smaller collection of shapes that are arranged in an interesting but not fussy composition.

'using the right plants in the right contexts will create a natural harmony'

Planting can also be used to create unity and harmony. Using the right plants in the right contexts will create a natural harmony. For example, consider how inharmonious a Japanese maple would feel in a desert-style garden. Plants have adapted in look and habit to their climatic conditions and this is one reason why they look right in their native setting.

'colour can be used to link the inside of the space with the outside garden'

Colour is a tool that is particularly useful in unifying a garden design. Colour can be used to link the inside of the space with the outside garden. For example, consider referencing the colour of a couch or accessories within the house in planting accents outside. Imagine how great a connection it would make if there were, say, a blue couch in the living room looking out onto a garden that had beds of plants in blues and purples.

SIMPLICITY: LESS IS DEFINITELY MORE

The saying 'less is more' is nothing new to most people. It is a statement that every designer has to remind himself or herself of time and again. It takes courage to edit things out that you don't really need. In the end, it definitely makes for a stronger design. The Persian Paradise gardens are a great example of how stunning simplicity can be. The simple idea of a central courtyard makes for a wonderfully uncluttered base idea and no matter how it is then carried out, the result will be restrained and elegant.

'it takes courage to edit things out that you don't really need'

At the start of this project you may be tempted to include every idea you've ever had for your garden. This is a good starting point, but then you need to learn to edit out the things that are not vital. This is actually really hard to do! That is why having a simple and distinct concept is so important. If you look back to the concept section on pages 90–91 you will see how the sample concept I came up with is really simple and does not include any overly fussy details. That is what you want as a starting point in a design, as too many design ideas makes for a fussy result.

SCALE AND PROPORTION: EXPLORING RELATIONSHIPS

There are a number of angles we need to look at in terms of scale and proportion.

- The relationship between the house and the garden.

- The relationship between the garden and the landscape.

- The relationship between the person and the garden.

The best way of getting this right is to start thinking in 3D, as it is very hard to comprehend gardens fully in a flat 2D way. Try and think about your garden in terms of heights. What is the tallest part of the space? A large tree? A wall? The house itself? Do they feel in proportion to each other? Does the space feel comfortable?

Consider the relationship between the house and the garden. Does the house feel too exposed or does it feel dwarfed by trees? Then what about the landscape and the garden? Does the landscape beyond feel as though it makes the garden itself disappear or alternatively does the garden overpower the landscape?

Similar thought processes apply to the person and the garden. For example, does the space feel comfortable to be in? Or are you dwarfed by the trees or walls? Are you too exposed in the space or maybe you feel crowded by too many elements around you such as groups of tall trees. A space that is out of scale in relation to the user can be a very uncomfortable space to be in, so it is important to study how the person and the space relate to each other and make relevant changes where needed. This may include cutting down trees where they are too tall, or maybe planting some new ones where they are needed to create height. If a high wall is too imposing in a space, then maybe the other side of the garden needs some added height to balance the space out, or perhaps the wall needs to be painted or have trellises applied to it to break up the size.

One very important thing to consider when you are designing with plants is how the scale of the plant will interact with the scale of the space. Think about how some small plants such as the ground-covering, low-growing varieties will enhance the height of the space and make it feel larger. Large plants such as large-leaved shrubs or trees, however, will be visually striking in your sight line, but can make the space feel smaller. This is a powerful tool to use in a garden design, but you have to be careful to use it in the right way. If your garden feels cramped and too small the worst thing you can do is use massive plants that further overpower the space. Getting the scale and proportion of plants to other elements in the garden right is tricky and often takes some trial and error. One of the main factors here will be striking a good balance.

'consider when you are designing with plants how the scale of the plant will interact with the scale of the space'

BALANCE

This refers to all elements of a design coming together in a pleasing composition. What I mean by this is that every element of the design should work well together as a whole. Consider a patio and some containers, for example. You will most likely not place all the pots in one corner. In most cases this would simply not make sense and would feel unbalanced. In the same way you will not put all the elements of a design into one place in the garden. All the elements should have a relationship to each other but also work in a balanced and well-rounded way.

The easiest way to achieve this is to create designs that have an inherent symmetry, as they have an existing mirror image balance. Examples of this can be found in many formal Persian gardens, as well as French or Italian formal gardens, where there is a strong element of symmetry and repetition, such as trees that are placed in the same pattern on both sides of the garden, or repeated shapes that are precise and mirrored in design. The risk in this perfectly symmetrical approach is that it can be a little boring, so extra care will be needed to make the garden unique.

'balance can be achieved by separating the garden into separate areas of purpose'

If you are drawn more to asymmetry and more organic shapes in the garden, then the space will not have that natural mirror-like balance and you will have to work that bit harder to achieve a balanced effect in the space. Balance can be achieved by separating the garden into separate areas of purpose. Think about which areas of your garden are best used for relaxing or sitting and which encourage movement. Each area will have to have a balance in size to all the other elements in the garden. For example, you won't give a simple path for walking more space than the patio area where you entertain, as this would be a waste of space and feel out of balance. Achieving a balance also means spaces in the garden need to relate to each other, feel comfortable and do not dwarf or elevate the user too much.

Balance will also deal with masses and voids, i.e. areas in the garden that are filled in and areas that are not. We often forget that voids such as lawns or ponds are also aspects that have a big effect on the balance of a garden space.

More Ways to Achieve Balance in the Garden

Balancing colour is a vital element of the design. You don't want a riot of colour in the garden at all times as this can cause the space to be unrestful. You also don't want a total lack of colour, as this may be boring. A good balance between green and other colours will result in a very naturally comfortable space that is easy to be in and will feel good for the user.

When it comes to light and darkness there will be an existing relationship between the two in the garden. Study if this is balanced already or if there are areas that need more light, either by planting or with actual lighting. You can also achieve areas of light by trimming trees, or create more shaded areas by planting trees or hedging, or setting up climbers or pergolas.

Mystery and excitement are also something that makes a garden a very vibrant place to be. I love a garden where you don't necessarily see everything on first glance, as this invites you to explore. This is a particularly relevant tool for child-friendly gardens. Creating different garden areas or garden rooms with views that hint of what is to come is a good way to create a sense of excitement and encourage people to explore the space.

WHAT HAVE YOU GOT? | it's not all roses yet

At this stage of the design process it is important to take a good look at your existing site. You must ascertain what your current space has to offer. What are its strengths and what are its challenges?

To answer this it is vital to look at practical factors such as garden aspect, climate considerations, existing boundaries, soil conditions and of course the measurement of your site. Before considering these practicalities, however, I like to look at the garden as a whole from somewhat of a distance. This is something you really should do for yourself. To begin, make yourself a cup of tea or coffee. I know, that sounds mad, but I can always think more clearly if I have a cup of tea in my hand. Once your drink is ready, take a chair, go out to your garden and sit down.

When you are seated, have a look around the site and have a think about your garden's strengths. Do you have an amazing view towards the sea? Is there a pretty wall? Does the garden get lots of light? Is there a small corner that has stunning dappled light and wild planting? There are bound to be strengths to look at in the garden. I truly believe it's vital to sit in the garden for a while and really experience the space while thinking about your garden's assets.

'nothing is unsolvable!'

Now consider your garden's challenges, those issues you must overcome to create your dream garden. I encounter many gardens that look like the garden on the right – completely uninspiring spaces that, on first glance, seem irredeemable. From badly drained spaces where the grass looks more like a pond than a lawn, to sites which are completely wild and overgrown with thorns, we are faced with many challenges when designing gardens. But nothing is unsolvable!

Some people refer to these negative aspects as 'weaknesses'. I prefer the word 'challenges' as I believe it makes the whole process of taking them on a little less daunting. I also think every challenge is an opportunity to make the garden more personalised and different. Indeed, the challenges of a site can often become interesting and unique focal points. For example, an old brick wall covered in ivy may become a great backdrop for a seating area. If not, perhaps you could screen it with something like a timber trellis or some tall trees. Think about how much that would improve the view. So you should look at any unsightly views you have and consider if they can become focal points.

> 'the challenges of a site can often become interesting and unique focal points'

When you've finished your drink make a list of the strengths and challenges within your garden. We will look at all this in more detail below, but I find writing things down is a wonderful way of getting your brain to process what you have seen and there is also the added benefit that it will now be a part of the decision process going forward.

Here's a sample list of strengths and challenges for a garden:

Strengths:

- Good views of the mountain beyond.

- Pretty old stone wall at the west side of the garden.

- Good morning light beside the back door.

- Lovely flowering shrub beside the fence on the east.

- Tall oak tree at the left back of the garden.

Challenges:

- A big puddle in the middle of the lawn.

- Dead tree at the back of the garden.

- Windy from the east of the garden.

- Oak tree blocking light to the sitting room.

ASSESSING YOUR SITE

Assessing your site correctly is an absolutely vital part of getting the design right. It is a bit of a fact-finding mission and will see you become something of a garden detective.

If you have been living with the garden for a while then you will probably be quite familiar with the plot, its strengths and weaknesses, etc. This can also mean that you may have stopped noticing certain things, such as annoying noise from a road, or good or bad views. In this case it is important to try to look at the site with fresh eyes.

'it is important to try to look at the site with fresh eyes'

In contrast, if you have just bought the plot then you definitely have those fresh eyes to look at it, but you won't yet have actual experience of how the plot works. In this case, you may need to research a little more. For example, if you have direct neighbours, talk to them about how they experience their garden. Since they are beside you they will most likely be able to tell you a lot about the conditions of your garden, such as if their garden gets flooded during heavy rain, or if they get strong winds from a certain direction. Look at how they have placed their seating areas and ask if it works for them.

It may also be a good idea to research the area. Are there any historical details or stories associated with the house or the area you live in? Is there a type of stone that is local to the area or trees that are native and can feature in your design? This is an important aspect to making your design sit right within its local context. It also brings us to the fascinating term *genius loci*.

Genius Loci

The first thing I like to look at when assessing a site is something called *genius loci*. This Latin term translates as 'the prevailing character or atmosphere of a place' and is something that has informed many of my designs in the past. It speaks of location, but not only that, it suggests that there is an inherent spirit to the site. The idea here is to let the spirit of the space guide you in the decisions you make about the design.

Let me give you an example. In a garden I did for clients of mine in Strandhill, Co. Sligo, the spirit of the space was so strong that it informed the whole design of the garden. The mountain Knocknarea, with all its historical and mythological associations, rose dramatically behind the garden and gave this space an incredibly strong elemental atmosphere that would have been not only foolish but plain impossible to ignore. Furthermore, the manner in which the vegetation of the mountain mixed with the majestic outcrops of rocks gave a feel that was so distinctly north-west of Ireland: dramatic, ancient and very natural. The views to the meadows

'the spirit of the space was so strong that it informed the whole design of the garden'

at the base of the mountain were also significant. As a result, the *genius loci* of the space became the focal point of the whole concept of the garden, which we named 'A meadow within a meadow'. The mountain was invited into the garden and the flowing meadow-style garden that we created bled into the wild meadow beyond, creating unity between the site and the surrounding landscape.

Not all gardens will have such a strong *genius loci*, of course, but when it comes to location there will always be something that informs the design approach. Look at the surrounding landscape, the city or town your garden is in. What are the influences from local history? What is the landscape in your area known for? What can you tap into that gives your garden a stronger sense of belonging to its location, as well as providing a deeper meaning? Are there stories about your particular area or old myths or legends that can excite the design process? I love this part of the process as it is a really fascinating fact-finding mission that is part-history research, part-dreaming.

Views

At this stage it is also worth noting down where the views in the garden are positioned. Remember, visual connections between the garden and the views beyond are just as important as views from inside the house. Sit in various places around the garden to make sure that you don't miss that slight hint of mountain or sliver of water in the distance. There may also be internal views in the garden worth noting down, such as areas of existing planting or boundaries that are worth looking at.

At this stage, also mark the bad views, making sure you know every visual that bothers you in the garden or beyond. Also make sure you remember these views are not necessarily the same in summer as in winter. A large tree may obscure an ugly wall in summer but leave it exposed in winter. Alternatively, a beautiful wall may be hidden by a climbing plant in summer but be exposed in winter. These are all important considerations when assessing the site.

Architecture

The next thing I always look at is the architecture of the building to which your garden is linked. This will most likely be your own house, although it could also be an old stable or a garage if the garden is removed from the house. Think here about the style of the house. For example, when was it built? Are there style connotations for the house and that period? For example, if the house is a small cottage, the design of the surrounding garden will need to take the architecture of the house into consideration. If your house is a sleek new concrete building, then the garden design should take this into consideration.

There are cases, however, where you can choose to contrast the garden with the house. For example, with a sleek contemporary house you could create a wildflower garden that is directly opposite to the house in style and yet could work really well — such as the spaces shown to the right and below by Noji architecture.

Here is another consideration. Are there elements on the façade of the house or on boundaries in the garden that may inform the style of the garden? For example, are there some wonderful curved windows that you could echo with similar shapes in the garden design? Or is the house made from a lovely brick that could become a material that you repeat in the garden, bringing the house and the garden together? The architecture of the house can be a really great starting point for a design, and if it is ignored the house and garden can become disjointed and the garden can feel wrong when the design is finished. The idea here is that you can use the house or structure to inform your design and give the whole scheme a great overall 'sense of space'.

It is vital to think about how we internally link the architecture to the garden. On a day-to-day basis most of us experience our homes from the inside-out and as

'think about how we internally link the architecture to the garden'

an interior architect and garden designer I find the idea of blurring the lines between inside and outside fascinating. I love how a house is totally transformed when we open it up to the garden by either bringing the garden in or the home out. For example, a window in the sitting room can be replaced with sliding doors, thus bringing the garden into your living space. Or you can extend your living space slightly by creating an outdoor room at the back of the house with large areas of glass and thus visually bringing the green garden in. Even a roofed or glazed pergola at the back of the house can really extend your living space and create a fantastic connection between inside and outside.

Orientation

Another absolutely vital part of assessing your site involves finding out its orientation. This is a crucial fact-finding mission as it informs how everything is placed in the garden. In our climate, patios or seating areas, for example, will need to be placed where there is direct sunlight to make the most of the sunshine that we do get. No one wants to sit in a shady, damp corner! Orientation also dictates what plants are placed where, as different plants have different needs when it comes to light.

In order to discover the orientation of your site you will need to find out where the north point is in your garden. A compass is the best tool for this. As part of the orientation, you will also need to look at the garden throughout the day.

'no one wants to sit in a shady, damp corner!'

Remember, the sun rises in the east and sets in the west so make notes during the day – or take pictures – documenting how shadows fall throughout a sunny day.

This will show you where the best areas are for seating, sunbathing and dining. This, in turn, will allow you to mark out areas for the things that don't need sunshine, such as utility areas for sheds, compost, etc. Do also remember that this will be different in the winter months as the sun is lower, giving longer shadows. It would definitely be helpful – if possible – to do a study in summer sunshine and one in the depths of winter.

Climate

Understanding the climate of your site and locality is one of the most important factors for your design. This will let you know what types of plants will thrive, where you can place what, and where you need screening or protection from the elements. One thing I always think of when designing in Ireland, for example, is that we are bound to have rain at some stage of the day on most days of the year. This is the climatic condition that makes Ireland so green, but also means spending time outdoors can be tricky. I always like to include an option of rain cover in my gardens so that you can be outside even when that inevitable shower occurs. Glazed pergolas, fabric awnings or open garden buildings are a great way of creating outdoor living spaces.

Your local climatic conditions must also be taken into consideration. Is the garden inland? Is it on the coast? What are the wind conditions? If you have been living in your house for a while you will most likely be pretty aware of the climatic conditions in the garden and will, for example, have been naturally drawn to the most sheltered and sunny areas.

> 'we are bound to have rain at some stage of the day on most days of the year'

You should also have a look at what is currently growing well in the garden. Are there areas where plants are drying up or simply not growing? This could mean that there is a dry, shaded area that you will need to either address through soil improvement or by planting shade-loving plants.

Another consideration is waterlogging (which we certainly have more of in Ireland than dry shade). Areas of lawn, particularly where soil has been compressed due to digger work during the building process, are often covered in moss due to bad drainage and will need to be improved. Some areas of a garden may just be damper than others and then you will need to decide whether you want to improve the drainage or use planting combinations that do well in damp or marshy ground, such as moisture-loving Iris varieties or Calla lilies.

Also consider how cold it gets in your garden. Gardens often create their own microclimates and your own space can vary from the temperatures given in a weather report. I have a thermometer in my garden, so I can gain an accurate account of the temperature on the site. The average minimum recorded temperature will definitely inform the plant choices for the garden, as frost can kill many plants. Talking to neighbours about what plant-life has gone well for them and any plants that have been killed by frost is a great way of finding out what works and what to avoid.

SOIL QUALITY

Looking at your soil quality is vital when it comes to planting. Finding out what type of soil you have is essential for getting an idea of what will grow on your site. Two main things matter here: the type of soil and the PH level. The PH level refers to how acidic or alkaline the soil is. PH levels vary from 0 to 14 and a neutral PH is 7. Anything above this number is alkaline and anything below this is acidic.

Let's look first at the structure of your soil to get an idea of what will grow in your garden. When you dig down about 10cm have a look at your soil colour. Ideally, what you want is a deep dark brown, loose soil with plenty of organic matter. Generally speaking, if the colour is a rich deep brown or black then it is most likely high in organic matter. If it is very black then this could be an indication of poor drainage. Soil can even turn almost slate blue, which could indicate bad drainage and waterlogging. Also, look out for any chalky white elements in the soil as this could mean it is chalky or nutrient poor.

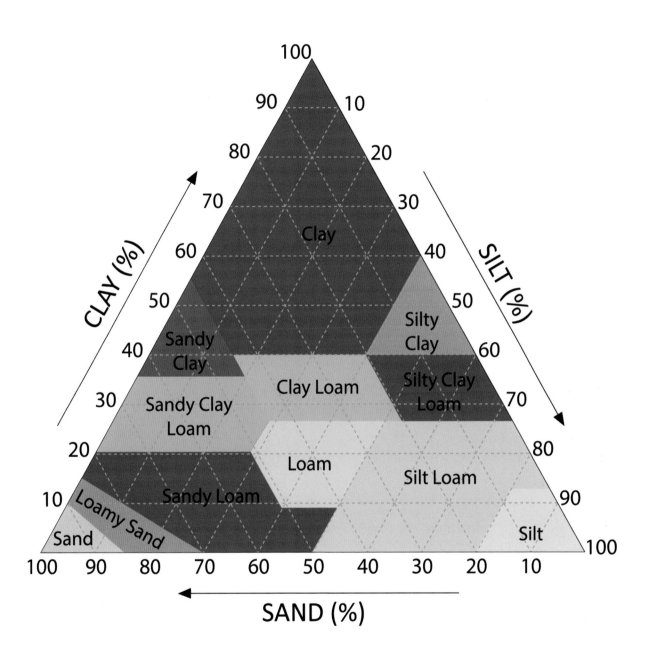

So What Type of Soil Do You Have?

Clay Soil

If your soil is finely textured and sticky to touch you have clay soil. It can even sometimes be rolled into a ball when wet. It holds nutrients well but may cause problems with waterlogging in wet conditions and cracking in dry conditions. This type of soil can also be hard to work with due to its high water content, i.e. it retains a large amount of water. Therefore, it should never be worked on when wet.

Sandy Soil

This soil will feel gritty to the touch and have lots of air spaces. If rubbed between your fingers it will fall apart. This soil will need plenty of sticky organic matter added to it as nutrients often get washed away due to the high air content.

Loam

This is a mix of clay and sand and is a great soil for most type of plants as it has good drainage but also retains the nutrients well.

Clay Soil

Sandy Soil

Loam Soil

Brown, gray and red silt soil

Chalk Soil

Peat Soil

Other Types of Soil

Silt soil is often a result of the erosion of rock and is a very fine soil that can cause damp conditions. Chalk soil is pale, shallow and free draining, but would benefit from having organic matter added to it. Organic matter loosens up soil as well as adding vital nutrients that are important for the growth of plants. In Ireland we often come across peat soils and this soil is rich in nutrients. Peat soil is also rich in humus, the dark-brown organic matter that is created when plant and animal matter decays. This is great for planting. Silt soil, in comparison, is generally acidic, which will limit what does well with it.

PH Levels: *Acidic or Alkaline?*

Every good garden centre sells soil-testing kits. These kits are a great way of finding out the PH levels in your garden. Remember different areas within your garden may have different levels, so try to test different areas around the garden. Make sure to label your results – and the relevant areas – in your notebook. I always use small sealable sandwich bags to collect my samples and write the areas on them in permanent marker. I would advise digging down about 10cm and taking a small sample from there as this will give the most accurate reading for your analysis.

When it comes to planting, the optimum PH range is generally 5.5 to 7, but there are plenty of plants that thrive in acidic soil, such as azaleas, rhododendrons and heathers.

'the key thing is to understand your existing soil well'

You can of course add materials to your soil to change its structure. For example, you can add lime to soils that are too acidic, and mix acidifying materials such as ericaceous compost to soils that are too alkaline. The key thing, however, is to understand your existing soil well, so that you know what will naturally thrive and what will not.

OTHER ASPECTS TO CONSIDER WHEN PLANNING YOUR DESIGN

I always like to retain as much original planting as possible in a garden and I have been known to design a scheme around a particularly strong existing focal tree. My feeling is that if a plant or tree is doing well and creating an ambience that is positive within your existing garden, then there would have to be a pretty strong reason to take it down. I remember that when I took part in RTÉ's *Super Garden* in 2012 as a competitor, there were two existing flowering cherries in the garden that became the backbone of the whole planting scheme. I did, however, have to move one of the trees as it just wouldn't work with the design where it had been planted and it ended up getting its own focal bed. Basically, the garden simply would not have been the same without those two trees. So my advice is this: think long and hard before you start tearing down existing trees, shrubs and flowers, as you may end up missing them when they are gone.

MEASURING YOUR PLOT

Although, as we have seen, there is a lot more to look at in the design process than the size of your plot, it is still very important that you have a good grasp of the space available for your design. Here is how to best measure your plot.

Measuring the actual plot can be a simple process or a very complicated one, depending on the shape of the plot. When it comes to measurements, if you are in a newly built house you may be lucky enough to have some architect drawings with which to work. These should generally contain the measurements of the site, a site plan and also have the dimensions of the house on the drawing, as well as where the windows and doors are located. In this case, you need to make sure you are aware of what scale you are working with. For example, when we use a scale of 1:100, every centimetre on a scale rule represents one metre in the real garden.

If you don't have the architect drawings to work from you may have to measure the site yourself. Getting this right is vital, as it will inform a lot of decisions in your design process.

First off, you will need to gather the correct equipment. What you need is a compass, measuring tapes, a scale rule, A3 paper and a pencil. (For more complicated plots you will need other equipment, such as pegs or bamboo canes, timbers posts and strings — which are important for terraced or sloping gardens — but let's stick to the simple rectangular plot for now.)

'measuring the actual plot can be a simple process or a very complicated one, depending on the shape of the plot'

The first step is to create a rough sketch of the whole plot on A3 paper. For the sake of your design I would recommend a scale of either 1:100 or 1:50 (meaning every metre in the garden is 2cm on the scale rule). It's best to do this to scale with the scale rule as this makes it much easier to measure. You can get a scale rule in any art supply shop. Also, you can get graph paper set out in 1cm squares, which can be very handy for this stage.

For a simple plot the measuring process is straightforward. Start by establishing a baseline, i.e. the starting point for your measurements. In most cases this will be your house wall, giving you a solid place from which to work. If you are creating a design for your back garden, for example, then you will start here by measuring the back wall of the house. This will be your baseline. For this you have to measure the wall length, the window openings, the door openings, the width of the poured concrete surround at ground level that many houses have, drainage channels, drainpipes and all other elements that appear along the house boundary. If you want to get a little more detailed here, then it would be wise to also look at the vertical measurements of the back of the house. It is always advisable to assess these a little as they will become important once you start looking at things like pergolas, trellises, climbers, etc., which may be attached to the back of the house.

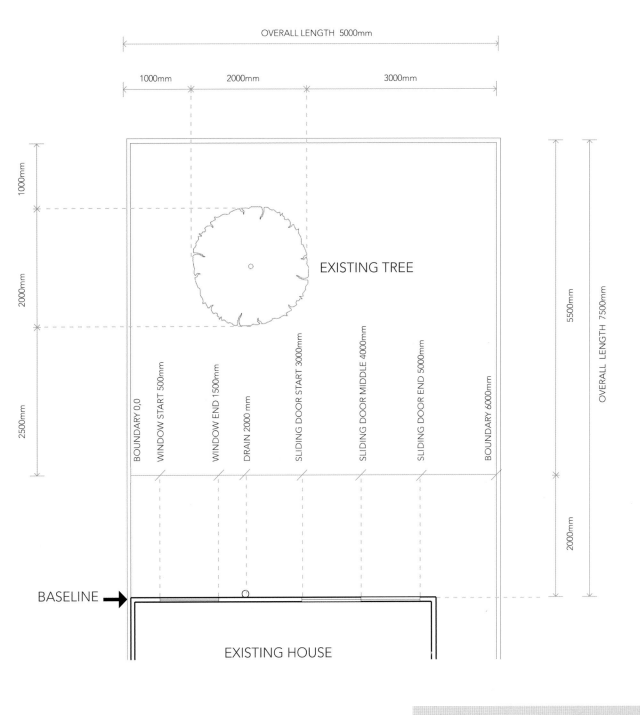

OVERALL LENGTH 5000mm

1000mm 2000mm 3000mm

1000mm

2000mm

2500mm

5500mm

OVERALL LENGTH 7500mm

2000mm

EXISTING TREE

BOUNDARY 0,0

WINDOW START 500mm

WINDOW END 1500mm

DRAIN 2000 mm

SLIDING DOOR START 3000mm

SLIDING DOOR MIDDLE 4000mm

SLIDING DOOR END 5000mm

BOUNDARY 6000mm

BASELINE ➡

EXISTING HOUSE

Site Measurements

Next, record all the boundaries of the site. I find that once you have these marked in, everything else gets a lot simpler to measure.

Triangulation

Another way to measure gardens to ensure precision is by using a process called triangulation. This is particularly useful in irregularly shaped plots. This is how to use triangulation to measure your plot:

1. Establish two points on your baseline. The two sides of the house are ideal. Name these Point A and Point B for clarity.

2. Now pick a point that you want to record – such as one of the boundary corners (say Point G) – and take a measurement from Point A to Point G. Also measure the distance from Point B to Point G. Note these measurements down.

3. Mark down all these measurements on your rough scale plan.

4. Do the same for the other boundary corners, as well as with any other existing features such as trees and sheds.

Once you have measured all sides of the garden and marked these measurements into your rough scale survey drawing, make sure you also mark all individual features into the plan, such as sheds, trees, existing hard landscaping, drainage, etc. You will also have to measure the heights of any features in the garden, like a shed, wherever possible. However, feel free to estimate something like the height of a tree. Make sure to add these measurements to your plan.

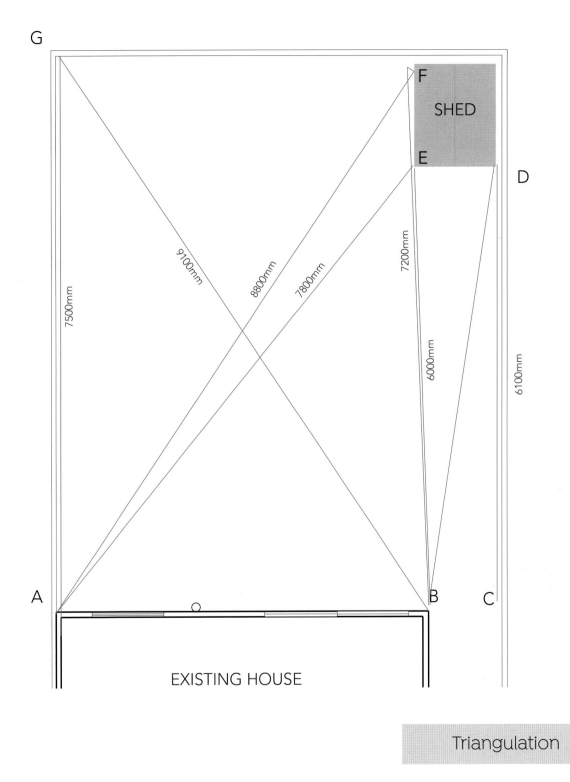

Triangulation

These measurements ensure that when you draw up your final plan to scale you can double-check your site plan against these triangulation measurements and all irregularities in the garden can be marked on the plan.

Off-set Measuring

When you have an irregularly-shaped boundary or feature in the garden there is another way of measuring this shape. This is called off-set measuring and for this you will need to establish a secondary baseline.

To do this lay a tape measure down along the boundary line at a ninety-degree angle from the house wall, i.e. the initial baseline. Now use a second tape measure to take measurements to the edge of the feature you are measuring at right angles from the first tape.

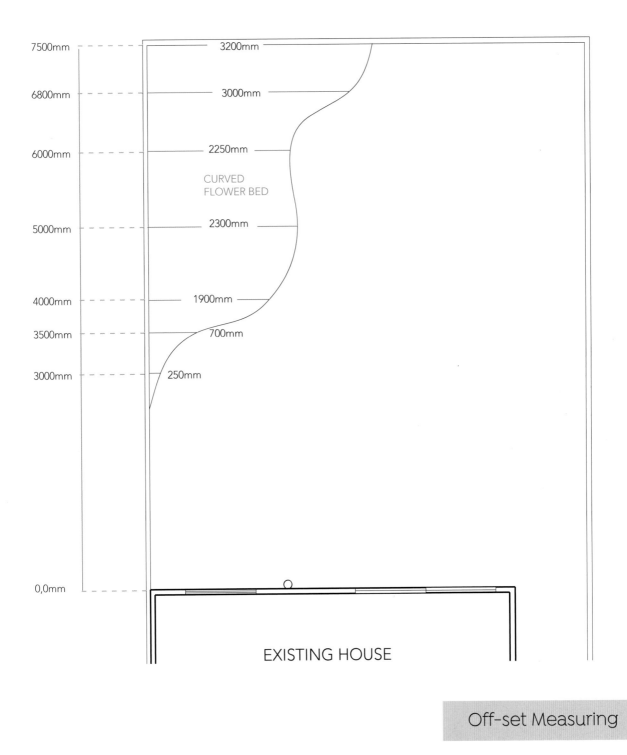

7500mm ···· 3200mm

6800mm ···· 3000mm

6000mm ···· 2250mm

CURVED
FLOWER BED

5000mm ···· 2300mm

4000mm ···· 1900mm

3500mm ···· 700mm

3000mm ···· 250mm

0,0mm

EXISTING HOUSE

Off-set Measuring

The Straight Timber Technique: A Simple Way of Measuring Changes of Level

For very large sites I would not advise measuring the site yourself, as this is a very complicated process and one best left to professional surveyors. For smaller gardens the straight timber technique is the simplest way of measuring changes in ground level. This means that you hammer four wooden pegs into the ground at 1-metre intervals as the ground falls, starting from the highest point in the garden. On top of these posts you place a 3-metre-long wooden piece of timber. The idea is to have these pegs hammered into the ground so that when the 3-metre piece of timber is placed on them it is totally horizontal. This will mean that the higher placed peg will be deeper in the ground than the lower one.

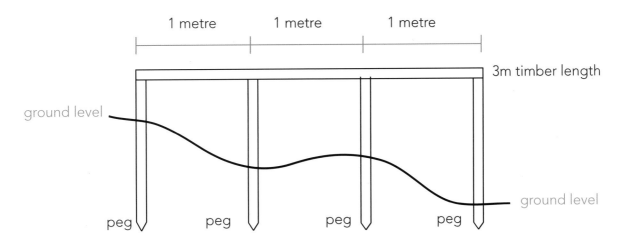

1 metre   1 metre   1 metre

3m timber length

ground level

ground level

peg   peg   peg   peg

You can check that the horizontal piece of timber is totally level by using a spirit level (a very handy tool used for measuring how level or straight something is). You can now establish the fall of the land by measuring the depth of the horizontal timber piece to the ground at each metre point. This is a very simple way of measuring the fall over a 3-metre length and can be repeated if the slope to be measured is longer than the 3-metre length. Simply start from the last post you measured and keep marking in the fall of the site until it evens out. You can also replace the timber length with a taut string, but the vital thing here is that the string remains very tight; otherwise the measurements will not be true.

FORM FOLLOWING FUNCTION | putting pen to paper

Personally, I go through many stages of self-belief and self-doubt during every project. Every designer I've ever talked to has suffered through the same waves of positivity and negativity. The process can be a bit of a rollercoaster. Finally putting pen to paper can be the hardest part, especially after so much research and measuring.

Thankfully there is an easy and almost fun way to approach this – we start by applying functions to the plan. This is a simple way to start drawing in the plan. You are not designing; you are simply marking what goes where in the roughest way.

This stage revolves around creating what is called the Functional Layout Plan (FLP). This plan ensures that all the functions needed in the garden are fulfilled. Have a look back at your day in the garden (see pages 22–23). What we need for this stage is the list of functional requirements that you made for your garden outlining everything you needed in the garden to make it work for you, whether it be a play area for the kids, a washing line, a rain cover or all three. Have your concept (which we covered on page 90) handy too; this succinct description of how you imagine your final garden should always be at your side.

Next you should sketch out the garden roughly on an A3 page. The easiest way of doing this is by getting some layout paper and tracing roughly over the measured site survey plan you created while measuring your plot.

With your functional requirements and con-cept in mind, it's time to start putting your functions into a site context. The idea here is to put the functions onto your plan so that you know exactly what needs to go where in order for the garden to function well for you. You can apply all your functions in simple, rough bubble formations as shown in the sketch on the right. This stage is important to do before you start thinking about shapes and what the garden will actually look like, as without this the garden just will not work properly on an everyday basis.

Think about where you want to place everything. So, suppose you need a large area for entertaining up to six people. This patio area should be facing the sun when you entertain (in this case you need to think about what time of day you are most likely to entertain. Evenings? Lunches?). You can now mark in this area on the plan. Make sure to draw it roughly to the size of the area you will need to fit six people sitting at a table with chairs.

Here's another example: you know you want a large area for the kids to play football. This children's play area will need to be visible from the kitchen window. Create a rough shape in a suitable area on the plan that represents the size you think they need for this.

'you are not designing; you are simply marking what goes where in the roughest way'

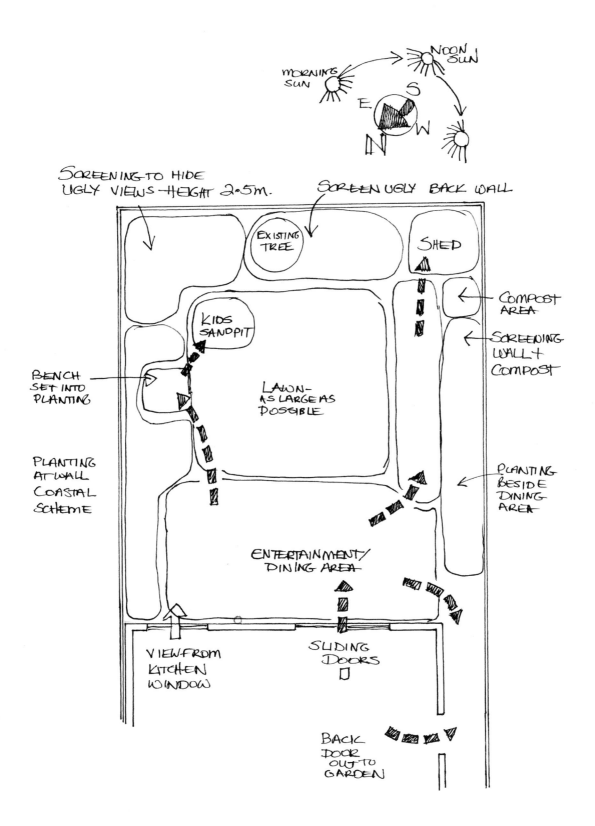

MORNING SUN

NOON SUN

E S N W

SCREENING TO HIDE UGLY VIEWS - HEIGHT 2.5m.

SCREEN UGLY BACK WALL

EXISTING TREE

SHED

COMPOST AREA

SCREENING WALL + COMPOST

KIDS SANDPIT

LAWN - AS LARGE AS POSSIBLE

BENCH SET INTO PLANTING

PLANTING AT WALL COASTAL SCHEME

PLANTING BESIDE DINING AREA

ENTERTAINMENT / DINING AREA

VIEW FROM KITCHEN WINDOW

SLIDING DOORS

BACK DOOR OUT TO GARDEN

The FLP is also is a great opportunity to mark in simple observations such as 'screening needed here', or 'soggy patch of soil in this area of the lawn'. All this will make your life so much easier in the long run. It also presents a great opportunity to resolve issues you have noted as your garden's strengths and challenges. Views, for example, should be taken advantage of by placing seating areas where they can be enjoyed. Screening can be marked for where bad views were noted in your site analysis.

Circulation is also an interesting aspect of the garden design that you can think about now. Consider where you enter and exit the garden, and how you would like to move through the site. For example, you can mark the route you would like to take from the back door to a potential seating area. This route must be easy to use and take into account the fact that you may be bringing out food or drinks from the kitchen.

'consider where you enter and exit the garden'

At this stage your FLP drawings will be very sketchy and rough. That's a good thing, however, as you will most likely have to do a few versions before you get the design layout right. The idea behind the FLP is to place all the things you need into a sketch of your garden, and to explore how they work together in the space. Once this process has been explored, and you are happy with the placing of all your functional features within the space, you will be ready to start looking at shapes for the garden design.

EXPLORING YOUR SITE THROUGH SHAPE

your design plan in layout

CHOOSING SHAPES FOR YOUR SPACE

What shapes you choose for your garden design will depend on a few things. First of all think about your concept.

Let's consider my sample concept again:

An elegant, symmetrical space that's calm and perfect for relaxation and entertaining. The style should have Persian influences and naturalistic planting that brings in wildlife, with an emphasis on using modern/contemporary materials.

All shapes in the garden will reflect your concept. The elements that can be taken from my concept include the strong geometric forms found in Persian-style gardens. Strong symmetrical lines will also bring this concept to life and the chosen shapes will most likely include symmetrical shapes, such as rectangles, squares and intersecting perpendicular lines, as found in many formal Persian gardens.

If, on the other hand, your concept is inspired by Irish mythology and wild naturalistic planting, then your shapes will most likely not have formal clean lines but the softer, curving elements that represent the natural Irish landscape and also bring Celtic designs to mind.

But what about a concept that brings two styles together? My Bloom in the Park show garden in 2012, which was entitled 'Cookie and Cream's Reclaimed Sanctuary', is a good example of this.

The concept there was to create an architecturally contemporary family garden made from reclaimed and recycled materials and combine them with wild naturalistic planting. The shapes were mainly strong clean squares and rectangles. These modern shapes of the hard landscaping were chosen to suit the shape of the site. They also suited the materials I was working with, which were quite industrial in style and worked well for clean, square shapes. The planting, however, which was unexpectedly loose and wild, was in total contrast to these contemporary, sleek architectural shapes. The element of surprise was that the mix of the industrial materials – I used scaffolding planks – worked so harmoniously with the wild and soft meadow planting. I think that really good design plays with the rules a little and at times uses contrasting shapes, thereby creating surprise and contrast.

'the materials worked harmoniously with the wild and soft meadow planting'

Next you should have a look at your functional layout plan. The bubbles and marks you have already created on this diagram may suggest some shapes for the garden. In my own designs this has often been a great starting point for planning shapes. That lawn area that you know you like in the centre of the design might be a large, circular space with everything else flowing off around it. Or the bubbles might suggest a series of square shapes that flow one into the next.

At this point it is vital to consider the design principles that we studied in 'What Makes Good Design'. Remember, the key aim of this stage of the design process is to create a composition that is balanced, harmonious, unified, simple and scaled and proportioned carefully.

WHAT SHAPE AND WHY?

A clever use of shapes is a great way of addressing awkwardly laid out plots. For example, if one of the challenges of the garden is that it is long and narrow, then shapes can be used to break up the garden into a series of smaller areas, making it feel less long. An example of this would be a series of circles or squares which intersect each other and lead naturally from one to the next, thus breaking up the long plot. Irregular-shaped sites that lack any clear shape can also be cleverly designed using a strong central shape that gives a clear focus to the space. This can then be supported by planting at the boundaries that makes the site appear regular, even if it is not.

'shapes are also a great way of introducing atmosphere into a garden'

Shapes are also a great way of introducing atmosphere into a garden. Flowing shapes, for example, give a feeling of movement and lend a natural feel to a garden, making it seem like it is an organically created space. Strong architectural shapes on the other hand give an ordered atmosphere and will give the space a more formal feel. Therefore, different shapes help create very distinct feelings to the space and we need to consider how to use shapes and how they make a space feel. Using one shape makes a strong statement, while mixing shapes and forms can be an interesting way of creating movement and interest in a space.

CIRCLES AND OVALS

The circle is an ancient form, gentle in shape and endless in nature, turning around on itself. It has strong spiritual and religious meanings in many cultures. Using this shape in the garden is a great way of creating softer central areas of interest. Often a circular central patio or lawn can look very impressive and suits both formal and informal schemes.

Ovals are a great way to create a more informal soft curve in a garden and are often more relaxed than the circle in feel. They can also add a feeling of length to a space.

A series of circle or oval shapes works really well in narrow spaces. They create separation within the garden but yet allow each circle to link to the next, creating a softly flowing pattern.

NOTE: When combining multiple circles we have to be careful that we don't create awkward spaces between the circles which are difficult to maintain. The sharp angles created when two circles meet are very difficult to pave and plant up. Even lawns don't do well in these sharp corners, so they should be avoided wherever possible. Leaving a space between the circles can be a way of avoiding these awkward shapes. Another consideration is that, by nature, hard-landscaped, curved spaces are generally pricier from a construction point of view than straight edges. For example, if you were creating paved areas in a circular form, then, due to the curving nature of the shape, there will be more wastage of cut stone or paving than in a square or rectangular-shaped area. The process is also more time-consuming in labour hours.

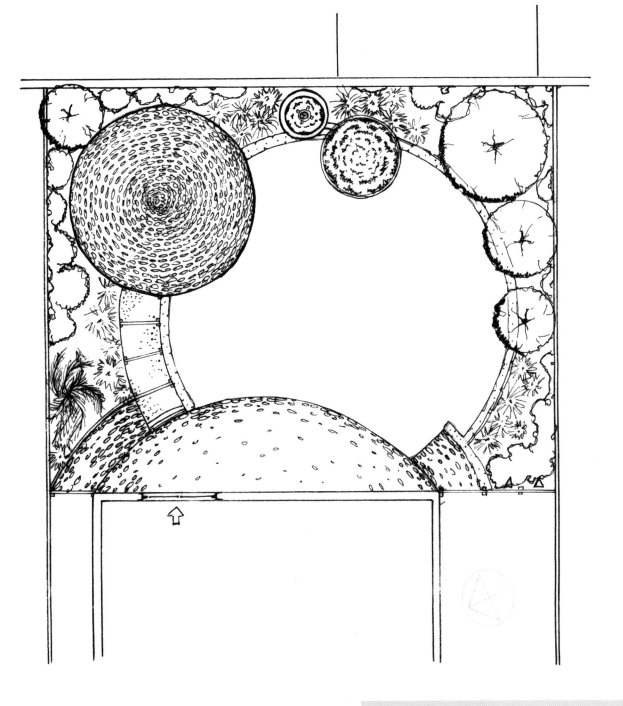

Circles and Ovals

SQUARES AND RECTANGLES

Squares are great for creating any garden style but are particularly effective in contemporary garden design. This is particularly true in urban back gardens, where it is possible (and very useful) to use a series of squares or rectangles to create different garden areas. These shapes can be used very formally in a symmetrical, central way or in a more relaxed way laid across the garden diagonally. Something that has always fascinated me – for a more informal approach – is how the formal lines of the square and rectangle can work together with inherently soft and informal lines of planting.

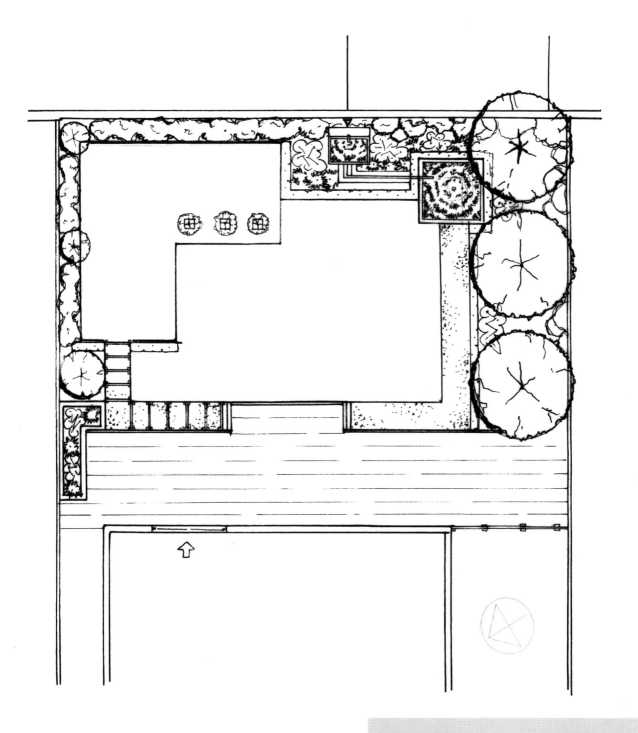

Squares and Rectangles

CURVILINEAR

The curvilinear shape combines circles and ellipses and uses sweeping arcs – not random lines – to create informal spaces. These are arranged using tangents, meaning that every shape has relevance to the other shapes in the space. Essentially circles are used here as an underlay and curving arcs are used to connect them. The curvilinear shape is a great option for informal spaces and creates movement in the garden. However, it differs from the free-flowing shape in that it is created using geometry rather than free-flowing hand-drawn shapes.

FREE-FLOWING SHAPE

This is a method that uses free-hand shapes to create mostly informal spaces. Basically these are free-flowing shapes that don't use rulers or compasses. It is actually the trickiest shape to get right. To do this successfully, without experience, I would suggest using circles and ovals

as underlying shapes and then soften the forms to make them more natural.

When you have drawn in the shapes you must make sure they have a relationship to each other. Do you need to add in pathways to lead from one space to another or do the shapes lead into each other on their own? Also make sure that the sizes of all the features are sufficient, e.g. paths need to be wide enough to accommodate movement, patios the right size for the table and chairs you need, etc.

If the shapes feel awkward, try out some others. You may well end up doing a few of these sketches before you get it right. I know I always do!

Try this:

Here is an exercise that is really useful if you are having trouble deciding on a shape. Sketch out your garden again by tracing over the FLP. Now think about your concept. What does your concept suggest you choose from the shapes above? Is it a natural scheme or is it formal? Choose the shapes that you feel most suit your concept.

Now take your FLP and overlay it with one page of layout paper. Sketch over the FLP and insert shapes based on this and your concept.

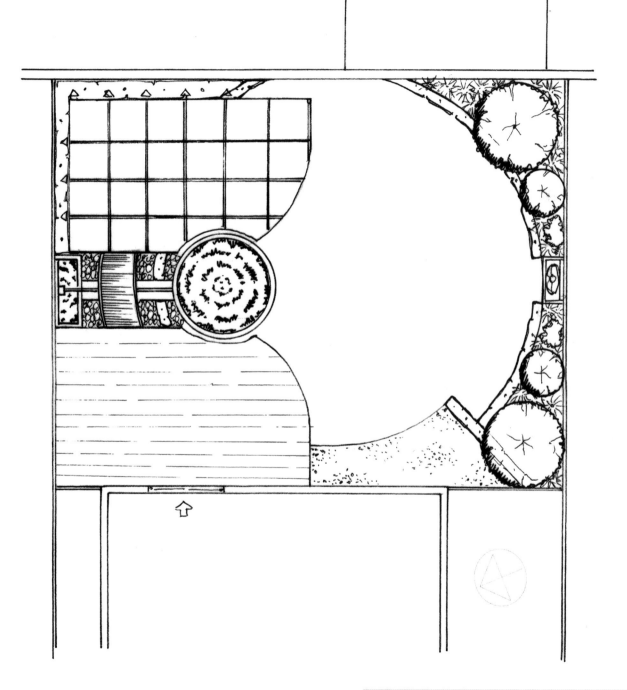

Curvilinear and Circle Mix

YOUR PLAN | fleshing out the design

Well done! At this stage of the design you have done a lot of the hard work. Your major decisions on function and layout have been made. You know what sort of shapes you want and have a sketch done of the garden. You have even outlined how you would circulate through the space.

It is now time to start fleshing out the garden with colour, materials and all the other vital elements that will give the garden substance. This is so much fun! Here we get to choose which colours best represent our ideas, we look at what materials work best for the concept and we also decide on the treatment of the boundaries of the site. We also have to think about lighting and of course planting, which is such a fundamental part of the design. Last but not least we will look at accessories. With all these areas there is one major rule to keep in mind – they all must match your chosen concept.

'it is now time to start fleshing out the garden with colour'

COLOUR: HOW WE CAN USE IT TO ENHANCE OUR CONCEPT

Colour can have a profound effect on our psychological experience of a garden. It can make a space feel larger and wider, or smaller and narrower. Combining colour in gardens is much like creating a careful artistic composition. The exciting thing about colour in the garden (as opposed to in interiors or fashion) is the ever-changing nature of plants themselves. As they grow, plants are constantly evolving in colour. Think about a hydrangea plant whose foliage begins as soft, lime green before maturing to deeper shades of green over time. Then a bud of lime green emerges, turns into a soft pink as it opens and finally gives an explosion of saturated, rich magenta in full bloom. This process of incorporating an ever-changing flower or plant into a garden design has always fascinated me.

> 'colour can have a profound effect on our psychological experience of a garden'

As a designer, much like an artist, one goes through phases of colours to which one is drawn. For example, when I started designing interiors I loved neutrals of whites and greys. After a few projects, however, I would find myself drawn to strong explosions of Prussian blue and teal tones. Having tried out most combinations, I can finally embrace the fact that all that matters is what colours make you feel happy right now, and what works for the design in question. Colour is intensely personal. No two people are the same, so colour choice will differ between each client and each scheme.

'green will always be the main colour in
your garden no matter what'

When it comes to the colour selection for your garden, it is best to start off with
the planting scheme. You have your base colours, i.e. your greens, which can
vary from deep, dark greens to limes and yellows. Green will always be the main
colour in your garden no matter what. I love green, with its infinite textures,
and it is amazing what you can do with a simple mix of greens with the odd
dot of colour. As green is also associated with the feeling of safety, fertility and
relaxation, it is no wonder that gardens make us feel good!

The plants you add after this green base should tell your story. What is it you
want to say in the scheme that you are creating? This goes back to the mood of your
garden and here it may be helpful to look at your dream diagram (see page 15). Do
you want to invigorate, soothe the senses or create a playful and fun composition?
Colours are a great way to bring these moods to life in the garden.

Things to Consider when Choosing Colours

Hot or Warm Colours

There are certain guidelines in garden design. One such guideline is that we tend not to incorporate more than ten to fifteen per cent of hot colours, such as reds, oranges and yellows – those at the top of the colour wheel – in a well-designed garden. The reason for this is that schemes can start feeling disjointed and stressful with too much warmth. In small doses, however, these warm tones are great for adding accents and highlighting focal point areas within the garden. They are very visually arresting and, when planted at the end of a garden, make that space jump out at you and appear closer and smaller.

'cool colours have a soothing effect on a person and can make a space seem larger'

Cool Colours

Green is one of the main cool colours in gardens, but a big range of blues, purples and lilacs are also considered cool colours. These colours have a soothing effect on a person and can make a space seem larger. Fascinatingly, in a 2011 survey conducted across thirty countries by Dulux, blue was found to be the world's favourite colour. It is no wonder it is so often used in gardens, as it works well with a broad range of colours, such as purples and pinks, as well as strong yellows and oranges.

Creating Moods with Colour

Colour is one of the best tools for creating moods within a garden design. What follows are a few examples of colour blends that I have used in my own work.

Elegance

For me it gets really exciting once we start mixing up the colours. For my Bloom in the Park Garden in 2012 my main colour palette was varying shades and textures of green. The idea of using a very soft and muted colour palette meant that the composition was easy to scan and pleasant to look at as a whole. I had the feathery lime greens in tree and shrub varieties of the Japanese maple, the deep earthy structural greens of the hornbeam hedging and the soft fluffy green of the grasses such as the Stipa *tenuissima*. What finished that scheme, however, were the dots of colour in-between the greens: spikes of Salvia in deep, calm lilac; dots of Aquilegia in maroon pink; swathes of light-pink Saxifraga *urbium* from my own garden. The amazing purple foliage of the 'Purple Emperor' gave it a little depth. The palette of cool colours was also represented in the hard landscaping of the structure, while the walls of deep purple and light lilac offered complementary hues to the planting. The understated colours created a calm space that was elegant and understated.

Contemporary Acid

The garden on the left features an exciting blend of contrasting colours and is very contemporary in feel. The colours come together to create a composition that is punchy and bold and will most definitely be noticed. It is a cheeky, almost neon mix of colours that are very modern and urban in mood. I always think schemes like this are almost like creating a planted version of graffiti: colourful, bold and youthful. The composition could be considered the opposite of a soft romantic scheme. Where a subtle romantic scheme might blend into the garden and give a calming feel to the space, here the scheme is eye-catching and invigorates. Sunset-coloured Echinacea *purpurea* 'Dreams Tangerine' flowers teamed with spires of lilac Russian sage (Perovskia 'longin') pop wonderfully against an acid yellow and lilac backdrop in this urban garden space. The effect is surprising: fresh and very modern. A great colour combination for the contemporary city garden. The acid yellow would work well on furniture or accessories such as cushions or tablecloths. Add in a few green sword-like leaves such as the evergreen Libertia *grandiflora* and you have a wonderful mix.

A Happy Scheme

This planting for a primary school in Sligo has a wholly different colour scheme. The warm orange of the external walls of the building acted as a starting point for the colour scheme. When it came to choosing planting, the evergreen Vinca *major* plant created a strong, evergreen backdrop to ground the scheme. On top of this a cheerful mix of yellow Primula *bulleyana*, purple spires of Nepeta x *faassenii* and cheeky pink Cosmos *bipinnatus* 'Dazzler' created a playful and fun take on the summer meadow. The colours chosen represent the fun, free feeling of childhood and aim to give a little feeling of happiness to the staff and teachers every day.

MATERIALS: USING MATERIALS TO BRING YOUR CONCEPT TO THE FOREGROUND

Materials, much like colour, have the ability to totally change the feel of a design. The balance of hard and soft landscaping (the vegetative materials in the garden, like plants, grasses, shrubs and trees) is an important one to get right and effective hard landscaping choices can really make planting schemes shine.

These materials are a vital part of our gardens. Think about it: paving creates easy circulation around the site; timber and metal can be used to create privacy, enclosure and provide shelter from the elements, and can also provide an important link between the house and the garden. The house is itself a structure that is purely 'hard landscaping' in character, so introducing hard landscaping materials in the garden that join together the garden and the house is a clever way of bringing coherence to a design. For example, a house may sit a little out of place beside a garden of purely lawn and shrubs and trees. By creating an area of patio just outside the back door, however, the transition from the house to the garden is softened and therefore feels like one has a more natural connection to the other.

The most important thing I have learned when it comes to choosing materials for the garden is 'less is more'. This goes back to our design principle of simplicity referenced in pages 100–101, where we talked about how important it is to edit out and choose everything in the garden wisely. There is nothing worse than too many materials fighting with each other for attention in a space. This creates a space that is disjointed and cluttered and will therefore be uncomfortable for the user. The rule is simple: choose two main materials.

The key to making the right choices when it comes to materials is to follow the concept you created. What materials will best represent the feel of the garden you are trying to achieve?

Let's take an example. Choose materials for this concept:

A calm, rustic coastal garden with naturalistic planting and small modern concrete art sculptures which is perfect for relaxing and entertaining in all weathers.

OK, so this concept already gives you lots of clues as to what materials you might use. The word rustic already tells you that the feel of the material should be informal and simple. The word brings to mind driftwood, old timber, natural stone and pebbles; materials that have been weathered over time and have a feeling of age and authenticity. You can, however, achieve this rustic feeling with many materials; they don't necessarily have to be as obvious as driftwood for the coastal garden. Indeed, the obvious choice may not be the best choice. For example, you could instead take old scaffolding planks and sand them to feel like driftwood. This would be an innovative way of using unexpected materials that are actually utility-based and making them fit your concept.

'the obvious choice may not be the best choice'

The one element in this example that sits slightly out from the rustic feel of the coastal concept is the addition of the modern concrete art sculptures. The use of contemporary materials in a rustic space can give the garden an added element of surprise, particularly where a rustic coastal garden may be somewhat clichéd. Introducing this material will bring the garden away from pastiche and help create something new and exciting. Of course, making the rustic and modern work together will be the key to getting the balance of the materials right. I personally love the combination of old and new – how, for instance, new concrete architecture can look placed next to soft driftwood material. The juxtaposition of two materials that are, in theory, opposites can be a very strong way of making each material shine.

Ground-Covering Materials

One of the most important choices for your garden will be what type of ground covering you choose in order to create a certain look or make it usable. Examples are stone, concrete, timber or gravel, but there are many more. This choice will be based on your garden's feel, your concept and the practical requirements you expect from your space. A family garden, for example, will have different material needs to a Zen meditation space. Practicality, safety, cost and style all play into the choices you make here. There are endless options, from decking to stone and gravel, and each has their place in garden design.

If you like the idea of having some form of permanent and solid ground-covering material in your garden, then a natural or man-made paving may be the best option. There are many options out there, from clever stone-imitation paving bricks to solid stone slabs.

When it comes to choosing how to lay our paving we generally differentiate between static and dynamic patterns. A static paving design will act as a neutral backdrop for the planting and features in the garden, and emphasise the space around it more. An example of this would be large slabs of limestone with little or no gaps between the slabs. A dynamic paving pattern, on the other hand, plays a more significant and eye-catching role in the garden. This style of paving will be more elaborate and will keep your eye inside the garden space or lead your eye to another part of the garden. For example, it may include designs such as pebble mosaics or zigzag designs. Basically, this makes a feature out of the paving itself.

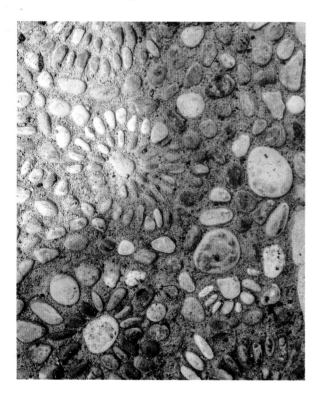

Both styles of paving have their place in garden design. Elaborate pebble mosaics, for example, can be used to create movement in a scheme and lead the user from one space to the next. Remember that these more elaborate dynamic pavings will emphasise the busy feel of a space and make it appear smaller. Therefore, they are better used in small quantities or in larger garden spaces. On the other hand, a linear or static paving style can be used to make gardens feel larger and create a broader sense of space.

When choosing your paving pattern you need to look at your concept again. All the materials chosen need to reflect the feel and style of your concept. Think about what paving material will best showcase your concept. For example, is your concept contemporary? Then you will either choose a material that reflects that approach, or you may use traditional materials, but use them in a modern way. An example of this would be to use 'traditional' brick, but laid in a contemporary design pattern.

Boundary and Fencing Materials

Choosing materials for your boundaries and fences depends on many factors. Firstly, we need to consider your setting. Is your site urban or rural? Do you want to create a sense of enclosure, or enhance openness and a connection to the views beyond? Site context and views will largely dictate what sort of solidity your boundary needs to have. In an urban context, security is another factor to consider. How we enter the space is a further consideration. Do we access the garden through the house or do we need to create some form of entrance/exit in the boundary?

One clever way of creating interest in boundaries is using a traditional material in a contemporary way. For example, although brick is often used in walling for traditional-style gardens, it can also be used in beautiful contemporary ways that result in an exciting mix of old and new. Bricks are generally considered a traditional material, but when used in a contemporary pattern these can become something totally new and exciting. This mix of old and new is a great way of designing spaces that are unexpected and challenge the perceived notions of what makes materials 'traditional' in our modern context.

Decking

Timber is another very popular material for the ground in gardens. Taking inspiration from warmer climates with New World styles, this is a wonderful warm material and is great for outdoor living spaces. Timber is a fantastic option for creating terraces or raising an area to the same level as indoor rooms. It is also often lower in cost than paving.

Here in Ireland a major factor to consider when choosing decking is the maintenance. It will need a lot of upkeep in order for it not to become slippery. Choosing a good quality, sustainable European hardwood such as beech, oak or birch is a good start. Then ensuring that you keep it clean from moss and leaves is key. There are also many new materials on the market that may be of interest for decking installation, such as artificial decking, which has come a long way in appearance and can be very long-lasting.

Soft Surfaces

Soft surfaces such as gravel, shingle, slate, bark or pebbles are a great way of creating contrast and interest in a garden. One of my favourite soft-surface features to use is a strip of pebbles as a drainage channel or edging beside paving slabs. This finishes off the slabs really well and makes even cheaper options look really well.

The key thing here is how you want people to move across this area. Pebbles can be a material that looks great but, unless set into concrete as has been done here on the left, this can be a material people don't like to walk across. Similarly, in order to make a successful pathway with gravel you will need to lay a base layer of mesh to stabilise it.

Bark mulch is a wonderful soft surface material that gives depth. I love seeing it used under trees in shady areas. It gives that really deep brown woodland effect and is beautiful surrounding ferns and bluebells.

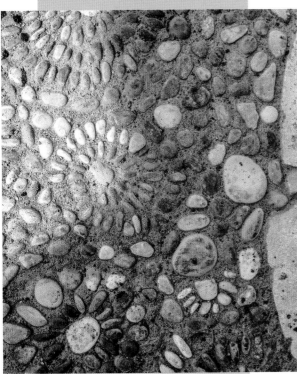

Re-Imagining Materials:
Bringing New Life to the Old

I am a big fan of experimenting with materials in my own garden designs. In my 'Cookie and Cream's Reclaimed Sanctuary' show garden we used old scaffolding planks and re-imagined them to create something totally new. Sanding this utility material until it was modern and smooth, we were able to use it to build structures and beds that were both contemporary and natural at the same time.

Another example was the 'Love Letter to the West' show garden at Bloom 2013, where my team and I spent a week and a half using blow torches to create a timber preserving effect called 'Shou Sugi Ban' for the boundary and hut in my garden. This ancient Japanese practice is a way of naturally preserving timber and, trust me, the effect is very different to just applying black paint to timber. The flames scorch the timber, creating a stunning silver/lilac hue on the black that you simply cannot achieve with paint.

As effective and beautiful as these processes are, they are equally time-consuming. This is a factor that is vital to remember when choosing what materials to use and how you want to treat them.

The Key to Re-imagining Materials

When choosing materials it is important to think outside the box a little. A clever use of unexpected materials can result in a really unique and fresh garden design. For example in this garden the designer, Cian Hawes, has used another industrial product – gabion walls – and made them work wonderfully in an urban garden setting. Gabion walls are more generally used in structural engineering projects when large areas of land have been excavated and the exposed landmass needs to be held in place. The walls themselves are wires of steel filled with stacked or randomly placed stones. This type of material is not one that you would normally expect in an urban setting, but the use of these as walls in show gardens and domestic settings has gained in popularity in recent years. Here the clever use of planting and mosses to soften the harsh lines of the product created a beautiful and homogenous result.

What is your Concept Material?

Once again, using materials that underline your concept is a good starting point. Let's take an example. For my garden entitled 'A Meadow within a Meadow' in Strandhill, Co. Sligo, we needed a boundary that reflected the contemporary and inventive nature of the house project and one that would do well in the salt-laden air of this coastal location. It also had to look natural to work in tune with the meadow feel of the planting.

The solution here was to use an industrial product – a reinforcing steel mesh – and fix it to a frame of black timber. This made for a fantastic growing frame, or garden trellis, for coastal roses and as it was rusted by nature the worry of maintaining this material with paint or other treatments was taken out. The colour is also a fabulous natural orange, which looks so at home in the meadow setting.

WATER: H$_2$O THERAPY

I absolutely love water in a garden. I live by a lake so am fortunate enough to look out at water every day. There is something uplifting and meditative about having water near your home. I think it has to do with the reflective qualities of the surface and the depth it creates in a scheme. We spoke about solids and voids earlier in the book and water is one element that creates a void in the garden. This element is instrumental in creating the sort of interest in a scheme that would not be generated by a simple, flat garden. Furthermore, as water reflects the sky and its surface moves with the elements, it offers ever-changing patterns and colours that make for a very exciting addition to every garden.

I am also a big fan of reflection pools, a shallow pool of water with no features like a fountain or fish to disturb the surface, such as this one in June Blake's garden in Wicklow. This is a wonderful solution for a courtyard or small city garden. It can really introduce depth by mirroring features surrounding the pool and can also enhance interest in a space. It is eye-catching and very calming at the same time. In this garden the corten steel water feature has been lined with black bitumen paint, making the water perfectly reflective and very effective as a feature.

Even smaller spaces can benefit from water and water features, such as a bubbling fountain or a trickling waterspout. These are a great and safe way of introducing water in family gardens. Even a small spout of water or a trickle coming out of a stone can be an exciting feature for children to explore without the risk associated with larger bodies of water. Children love playing with moving water, and safe water features that they can touch are a delightful addition to a family garden. Water features like this can also often have a pleasing sound in a city scenario where you have traffic and urban noise. In fact, if used correctly, these water features can effectively overpower the sounds of the city. Flowing, splashing, trickling – all these sounds can be particularly therapeutic and relaxing in an urban setting.

LIGHTING: BRINGING LIGHT TO YOUR SPACE

Many people don't view lighting as an important aspect in a garden design. However, consider this: without lighting your garden does not exist at night. In most cases it will simply blend into the shade once darkness falls, making it difficult to use safely and effectively.

The first thing to consider for those who see lighting as essential for garden design is this: what do you need the lighting for? Think about what you will be doing at night in the garden. If you are entertaining, for example, will ambient, glowing mood lighting be enough for dining with your friends or will you need specific lighting for, say, barbecuing or an outdoor kitchen area?

Once you have thought of your potential tasks, you must then consider safety. For example, are there steps that need to be illuminated to make them safe at night? Do paths need to be edged with a series of lanterns to ensure that the user is led down to a specific area?

'looking out at your garden at night can be a very exciting thing'

One of the most vital reasons to consider lighting in your garden is to retain the inside-outside connection at night. Looking out at your garden at night can be a very exciting thing: observing the colours change and the textures become more apparent. I love expanses of colourful, painted walls softly lit at night to become a backdrop of light for plants. Lighting also brings atmosphere to a garden, highlighting strong features and creating areas of warmth and glow.

A combination of ambient glow, safety and task lighting, and even clever candlelight, will be a great way of making the most of a space, particularly for people who like to entertain in the evenings and at night. Another effective source of light could be a fire pit, which is a great draw for people at parties and gives such a beautiful warm light to a garden space.

Choosing light fittings will be based around your concept and your other chosen materials. For example, if you have chosen black timber with copper details as a boundary in the garden, then lighting in a copper colour or casing would be an elegant and fitting choice. If your materials are very modern, with elements of concrete and stainless steel, then perhaps clean contemporary stainless steel lighting fixtures will work best.

In many cases the actual fittings can be hidden, allowing the actual light or the focus of the light to be the star of the show. An example of this would be a hidden LED uplighter illuminating a tree or shrub. Here the plant is the star.

'choosing light fittings will be based around your concept and your other chosen materials'

PLANTING: DESIGNING WITH PLANTS

Planting is the feature that can make your garden truly great. I think there is no better way to really customise your space than with planting. But first it is, of course, essential to consider the practical points in your garden space. Look at your site analysis. This will tell you where the shade in the garden is, what type of soil you have and ultimately which plants will do best in the site and where they would be best placed. This site analysis is a valuable tool to make sure you don't make mistakes that end up costing you when it comes to planting.

'there is no better way to really customise your space than with planting'

Another very important factor to consider before you start designing with plants is of course the maintenance level required of your garden. How much time exactly are you willing to put in to the maintenance of the plants? This will have a major impact on what type of plants you choose and how you enliven the space with plants. A lower maintenance garden may have more evergreen plants such as structural hedges or evergreen shrubs and trees, but a factor to consider here is that there may be an added cost to slower growing plants (this added expense is due to their taking longer to get established at plant nurseries where the plants are grown for retail garden centres).

A Concept-driven Planting Style

When approaching the design of a planting scheme there are many methods to consider and over time every designer finds their own preferred way of choosing plants. In most cases, however, it is best to base your planting choices around the concept. With that in mind you can start the process of picking combinations of plants that suit the concept. The chosen plants should therefore reflect the style, but also be placed in the planting beds to mirror the way they would grow in the scenario on which the concept is based.

> 'the chosen plants should reflect the style and mirror nature'

Let me give you an example. With a soft meadow concept the plants would be chosen to represent what would grow in a meadow, but they should also capture the manner in which they would grow in that environment. You would therefore not plant these meadow plants in straight formal lines but rather in scattered, loose and informal drifts. Both the plant choice and the planting pattern become representative of the meadow style.

Another example would be if your concept were a contemporary space with a modernist feel. In this case block-planted shrubs and strong architectural forms of hedging would be a good starting point.

So consider your concept idea. Think about what it means in terms of feel and visuals. Then look to emulate this pattern in as authentic a way as possible.

My Planting Approach

My own style of planting is somewhat naturalistic even when combined with, say, more formal clipped hedging for structure. Over the years I have started to approach most planting designs with these main approaches in mind.

The first thing I consider is the base plant. This will be a plant that has the most impact on the scheme and is one that really shines and has a visual appeal. Think about using plants like the soft yet visually arresting catmint as the base plant and combining it with another similar-textured one, such as a more pink variety of the Salvia family. This gives a strong statement of colour and yet they are soft enough to create a texture and feel across the space.

What we need now is a unifying plant. If you are going for a more naturalistic scheme here you can introduce masses of deciduous grasses, which give that real meadow feel, and these will then die down in winter when the garden becomes dormant. Evergreen grasses or plants, such as those of the Libertia family, can be very strong plants to unify the scheme. Many garden schemes can benefit from having a strong plant that gives evergreen structure throughout the year and the unifying plant could be lavender, for example, or euphorbias, both of which are great green unifiers.

Next come the so-called 'scatter plants', which give a real sense of wildness. These plants are scattered throughout the scheme and unite the whole area just as plants would that were grown in a wild habitat. I love plants such as echinacea and how, when used carefully, they look like they have always been there. The tall seed-heads also work wonderfully in contrast to the colours of the primary plants.

In addition to the above, I like to include plants that become what I call the 'star plants'. These are the plants that will undoubtedly be noticed by everyone looking at the garden. As they are so striking, however, they need to be used sparingly in order to avoid the scheme feeling overpowered. Think of a single stunning peony rose bush, with flowers that float above all the other plants and really draws the eye. Or a cluster of colourful iris flowers that lift ruffled heads above the other plants. These plants are the star or feature plants and they should really speak of your concept, pick up on chosen colour schemes and, in doing so, help create the wow factor.

Most gardens will take a while to establish themselves and nature has a way of making sure planting design is never predictable, but this is part of the fun of garden design. Even in the best-designed planting schemes there will be surprises in terms of some plants doing better than others, schemes changing over time and interactions with adjacent gardens – such as when plants self-seed. That's what makes gardens exciting and fresh, the fact that they are part of an ever-changing cycle.

'nature has a way of making sure planting design is never predictable'

Planting through the Seasons

We must not forget that the garden is an ever-changing space. With every season we see a new face and it's important that we organise the planting around this. My advice would be to do a planting calendar such as the one below when you plan your planting. This is a great way of charting when certain plants are in flower and ensuring that there are no gaps in the planting year.

For some exciting planting schemes have a look at my ideas in the case studies on pages 210, 214 and 219.

	JANUARY	FEBRUARY	MARCH	APRIL	MAY	JUNE	JULY	AUGUST	SEPTEMBER	OCTOBER	NOVEMBER	DECEMBER
Hellebore Lady series												
Iris siberica												
Lavandula hidcote												
Anemanthele lessioniana												
Sedum matrona												
Achillea 'Lilac Beauty'												
Acer palmatum												
Vinca minor Double Bowles												
Narcissus 'Carlton'												
Crocuses												
Geum Princess Juliana												

ACCESSORIES: THE FINISHING TOUCHES

One of the most effective ways of bringing your concept to full fruition is the final addition of design accessories. These are more changeable and can even be replaced to create different ambiences if you get sick of one scheme or item. These include items such as cushions, ceramics, freestanding containers and, of course, freestanding furniture. Small, movable water features and fire pits can also be considered design accessories and can be very effective additions to the garden.

The one major guideline here is, once again, less is more. Only choose items that are absolutely vital and leave it out if the accessory does not suit the concept.

Basing your choice of accessory on the concept is the best way of ensuring that you get the accessories right. In my own garden designs I treat accessories as an integral part of the design process from the very beginning. They form a strong atmospheric base to the space and are as important to the big picture as the rest of the design. This is why I always take time to consider how all accessories can be incorporated or even customised to go perfectly hand-in-hand with the concept. Furniture made from the same material as surrounding structures, or small sculptures made from the same material as bordering gates can bring unity to a space and underline a concept material.

Custom-made cushions in a colour scheme such as the ones here are a great way of echoing the concept. Or ceramics created for the space in the chosen colour scheme are a great way of picking up on colour and bringing the eye through the space.

Custom-made sculptures are another fantastic way of picking up on a concept. The wonderful timber creation in the top picture here is a strong way of reflecting the industrial concept and ethnic style of the garden designer.

CONCLUSION

Having looked at all the different elements that add up to a well-designed garden, we can see how important each element is in creating a coherent and visually pleasing garden. Not only that, these are all elements that ensure the garden is also a perfectly functioning one for you, that ultimately is easy to use and a pleasure to be in.

The great thing about taking on a process like designing your own garden is how personal the end result will be. Every detail is going to be 100 per cent your style. This is something very special.

It is also a very rewarding process. Whether you take on the whole garden or just small areas using my outlined process, I know how good it will feel when you see the results of your labour.

You will have achieved something wonderful for yourself: your very own dream garden.

CASE STUDIES

CONCEPT CASE STUDY 1: 'COOKIE AND CREAM'S RECLAIMED SANCTUARY'

The Brief

The client was a family of four with two young teenage children who took part in RTÉ's *Super Garden* in 2012. The family loved entertaining and wanted a space for dining and relaxing in the garden. They also had two beautiful rabbits, Cookie and Cream, who needed to be taken into consideration when thinking about the prospective space. The site used to be a meadow before the estate was built. The family was open to using unusual and innovative materials.

The Concept

A contemporary space using modern materials that contrasts with the soft, naturalistic, meadow planting. The garden is based around family life and the two pet bunnies. It should be great for entertaining and relaxing, as well as having an innovative use of materials.

Materials

Materials here saw us using old industrial materials and treating them to become something new. Scaffolding planks were used to create everything from the hut to the seating and using just this one material brought great unity to the space. The hut was created using two large reclaimed teak doors, combined with re-imagined scaffolding planks. Leftover corten steel sheets from an architectural project became wonderful eye-catching works of art on the wall of the garden and brought texture and depth to the space. These gorgeous rusty panels will just get better with time and are one of my favourite materials in the garden.

Treatments

All timber areas were finished with an organic paint from Germany called AURO and custom mixed in a pale lilac for this space to create a semi-transparent wash of colour so that the grain of the timber was retained and yet the material was protected from the elements.

Colour

Colour in this garden was fairly limited and yet had a strong impact. The contrast of the rich purples of the walls and greens of the planting were chosen to underline the contrast of architecture and nature. Swathes of white in the planting and dots of light yellow were used to bring lightness to the scheme and a scattering of maroon-red created little elements of unexpected colour in the overall picture.

Accessories

Here the accessories were kept to a minimum. The steel wall features became accessories like a painting would in an interior space. The large solid blocks of timber were the only furniture that was not permanently installed and instead became seating that acted as focal points. The most elaborate and eye-catching accessories were the customised cushions by designer Ana Faye, which took the colours of the garden and used fabric and leather to create a stunning, complementary design. The shapes were designed to mirror the geometric shapes of the garden and this finished the space perfectly.

Planting

Planting was based on a meadow. As the site had originally been a meadow before the house was built, I wanted the planting to reflect that. I started the whole scheme with the trees. I wanted a strong, rich, yet fluffy green in the garden as a base colour and Japanese maples did exactly that. A line of hornbeams as a hedge created a wall of green on the right side of the garden and became a contrast to the purple colours of the wall.

Grasses were one of the main starting points for the garden. Stipa *tenuissima* is a wonderful deciduous grass that has fantastic movement in a scheme. The next plants I chose were Lavandula *angustifolia* 'Hidcote' and Nepeta *x faassenii*, which featured strongly throughout the garden and became a central backbone of the scheme as they gave it a little solidity, especially as a meadow scheme may be too loose on its own.

Spires of Salvia *x sylvestris* were chosen to bring a vertical element into the raised planters where the grasses were based. The form of these Salvia contrasted nicely with the grasses. Achillea *credo* was used to again underline the meadow feel of the garden and bring umbellifer shapes into the planting design. Umbellifer-shaped blooms are ones which grow in 'umbel' forms – essentially the shape of an umbrella. These shapes are very effective for adding interest to the higher levels of planting combinations. Then we had structural Sedum 'Purple Emperor', which also had the added benefit of bringing the colour purple into the foliage of the scheme.

The light yellow scattering of Trollius *x cultorum* 'Alabaster' really made the scheme pop and gave it lightness, while the white fluffy heads of the Lychnis 'White Robin' plant appeared to float above it all. At the front I included home-grown Saxifrage *urbium* to pick up on the white at the back and these created lovely areas of lower evergreen cushioning with soft white-pink flowers floating above them. To finish off the top of the wall I used purple Clematis 'Polish Spirit' climbers to create a cascade of blossom and soften the edges.

The Result

A space with strong architectural detailing combined with soft planting that became a space for the family to relax and entertain. The inclusion of indoor and outdoor spaces meant the garden could be used in all conditions.

The special thing here was how the bunnies were given their own space in the same style as the rest of the garden and even had underground tunnels from which they could access their little hut made from scaffolding planks, with glazed panels for them to look out.

CONCEPT CASE STUDY 2: 'A MEADOW WITHIN A MEADOW'

The Brief

The clients, who run the popular Shells Surf Café in Strandhill, Co. Sligo, had just done up an old cottage at the base of Knocknarea in Strandhill. The feel of the cottage was a great mix of industrial style and innovative vintage touches. The garden needed to create a connection between the views beyond and bring the garden and views inside the house. An outdoor shower and surfboard storage area were also important parts of the brief.

The Concept

A naturalistic-style garden with industrial elements that works well for the coastal setting and brings the inside together with the outside.

Planting

The grasses here were a very important part of making the scheme fit in with the meadow views beyond. I chose a variety of grasses such as Stipa *tenuissima*, Stipa *gigantean* and Anemanthele *lessioniana*, the latter giving a little evergreen colour in the winter months. Stipa *tenuissima* is one of my favourite grasses to give movement to a scheme and Stipa *gigantea* has wonderful tall plumes of feather flower heads that rise above all the other plants in late summer and autumn. Libertia *grandiflora* has lovely sword-like leaves that bring a little more green to the scheme.

When it came to colour selection I started off with the beautiful Astilbe 'Purpurlanze'. A stunning pink plume of flowers reminiscent in shape of the native meadowsweet, this plant has valuable seed-heads in the lean months of winter. This is important for wildlife when there is very little food in the landscape for animals and birds. Iris *sibirica* and Papaver *orientale* were lovely early summer accents in the garden and the Sedum *herbstfreude* ('Autumn Joy') and Achillea *millefolium* ('Lilac Beauty') became the stars of the autumn garden.

Finally, Verbena *bonariensis* was chosen to float elegantly over all the other plants and the purple head of the beautiful Giant Hyssop was a great way of introducing colour without losing the meadow feeling.

Materials

The choice of materials for this garden was one thing that I thought long and hard about. Any timber chosen had to do well in the salt-laden air of the west of Ireland and the chosen metals had to be able to withstand the winds and salty rain. We chose cedar wood as the material for cladding the house and for the storage solutions, as it deals well with coastal climates and turns a beautiful silver-grey after some time exposed to the elements. The metal we chose was an untreated rusted steel mesh that we allowed to stay in its natural form rather than paint it. Pebbles and gravel were also chosen to reflect the coastal nature of the location.

Treatments

Most of the materials in the garden were allowed to stay in their basic state. For example the cedar was simply left to grey up over time and the steel allowed to rust. The thought process behind this was based on my experience of the climate in this location and being aware that metal will inevitably rust and timber will basically be sandblasted by the strong Atlantic winds. Instead of fighting this, we used it to our advantage.

Colour

The materials in this garden were really secondary to the drama of the views beyond and we wanted to make the garden feel as open to this landscape as possible. This meant painting some of the necessary fence posts black to make them disappear into the landscape. The natural feel of the meadow beyond inspired the colour palette of the planting in this garden: dusty greens, lime greens and the odd rise of deeper green trees.

As this garden was a domestic dwelling it was important to have some colour surrounding the very modern house, so we chose a simple scheme of purples and rich pinks that emerge throughout the year. This meant that the colour was not too strong for the location and the garden would still allow the landscape beyond to bleed into it in a natural way.

Accessories

The stylish owners of this garden have a vast collection of carefully chosen accessories inside the house and so, for the garden, we decided to keep it simple. The rustic fireplace and outdoor shower were the main accessory features. Small items of rusty metal were also found during the excavations on site and hung up on the wire mesh.

The Result

A softly sloping and controlled meadow-style garden sweeping up to meet the real meadow beyond. Storage for surfboards was integrated into the house cladding and an outdoor shower looked out onto the mountain views behind the house.

CONCEPT CASE STUDY 3 :
'A LOVE LETTER TO THE WEST'

The Brief

This show garden was designed around a part of the world that is very special to me. The brief was to design a garden with a small roofed structure to represent the north-west of Ireland and try to replicate the feeling of this beautiful landscape in a show garden setting. It also had to show the 'New Ireland' and therefore have elements of surprise.

The Concept

A calm space that shows the landscape of the north-west of Ireland in a unique way.

Materials

The materials used in this garden were a simple pine timber, which we re-imagined to become something totally fresh and new by a practice called 'Shou Sugi Ban' (outlined below). The only other hard landscaping element we used was Kilkenny blue limestone, which created a stunning contrast to the black timber and had some beautiful fossil inclusions in the stone.

    Water became a strong element in this garden and the natural water feature was used to represent the many lakes of the west of Ireland as well as give the garden a sense of scale and proportion. The little timber dock over the void of water was a great place to dangle your feet too!

Treatments

We scorched the timber using blowtorches, a practice called 'Shou Sugi Ban' (see also page 190), to create a blackened effect. It aids in preserving the timber and keeping it from rotting. The most surprising thing for me was how utterly beautiful it made the timber. This treatment is so effective, creating a subtle, almost silver-purple hue on wood.

Colour

Colour here was very limited. I love the depth the dark timber gave to the scheme. The colour black is great for making boundaries disappear where needed and allows the planting to really stand out. When used in the timber structure and the furniture the black worked well with the pink and purple accessories and turquoise copper detailing. The hut was also elaborately designed and scorched, creating a very cosy place to relax and enjoy the views. I chose the black for a variety of reasons but one became very apparent as the design went up and the planting went in: it allowed nature to be the star of the show.

Planting

The planting here aimed to be a representation of the nature in the west of Ireland. Trees were all native varieties such as birch, beech and willow, and went from shadier areas to the wetter bogland areas near the pond. Rocks and mosses formed a dense woodland environment under the trees. The main planting beds to either side of the hut were my favourite part of this garden, though. Bursting with green and flecked with purples and pinks, this scheme is one of my favourites.

I started with my favourite grass again – Stipa *tenuissima* – and built the remaining plants around that. One thing the west of Ireland is so known for is the beautiful foxglove, and the spires of the magenta pink Digitalis *purpurea* variety were integral to my scheme. Next came the sword-like leaves of the iris. I chose a stunning black iris here – the Iris *chrysographes* 'Black-flowered' to reference the dark background with its subtle shimmer of purple. Varieties of tall Knautia *macedonia* created little pincushion accents above all the other plants. The addition of lupins, which had a graduated, almost ombré feel, brought an added interest to the scheme and echoed the spires of the foxgloves.

Accessories

The aim in this garden was to use only materials from the north-west of Ireland wherever possible and also labour and designers from the region. This also meant that accessories had to be created by local artists and craftspeople. My design for the chair and small table in the hut were custom-made by the master craftsman Charles Perpoil, who specialises in custom furniture and carpentry and is based in the west of Ireland. Other accessories included custom-made cushions from Foxford Woollen Mills wool fabric and cosy throws to match, as well as candles from the north-west-based VOYA brand. We also included ceramics from ceramic artist Ian Carty.

The Result

The concept was brought to life using innovative material treatments teamed with naturalistic planting. Timber was burnt to preserve it and reflect the feel of the deep, dark bog landscape of the west. Planting surrounded a calm pond at the front and bled back to grow into shadier areas of native planting.

An interesting additional part of the brief was to rebuild the hut at a lake in Co. Leitrim. This was a great way of making sure the show garden — which was only there for the public to see — found a permanent home in the west of Ireland. The rebuild was a great event in which the whole community got involved.

ACKNOWLEDGEMENTS

Thanks a million to everyone involved in making this book a reality. First of all to everyone at Mercier Press, especially Mary Feehan, who, over delicious coffee and cake at Ballymaloe House, let me tell her about my vision for the project and subsequently took it on. Thank you. To my editors, Noel O'Regan and Wendy Logue, and proofreader Bobby Francis, without whose support the stories in this book would have made a lot less sense – it has been a pleasure. Thank you Sarah O'Flaherty for your patience with the endless files of pictures and bringing the book together in a coherent and beautiful design. And last but not least thanks to Deirdre Roberts for the great chats, her enthusiasm and guidance. At the Lisa Richards Agency I would like to thank my literary agent Faith O'Grady for her valuable advice and assistance.

Thanks to Philip Kampff and all at Vision Independent Productions and the whole RTÉ *Super Garden* team. Thank you to Ruth Brett and Emer Cobbe and all at Woodies Ireland, and to Gary Graham, all at Bloom in the Park and Bord Bia, as well as the great Bloom garden designers whose wonderful work features in these pages.

Many thanks to the talented designers and architects who were kind enough to send me images of their work for this book – especially June Blake, James and Helen Basson, John Monahan of NOJI Architects and Roisin Lafferty of KLD Designs, as well as to all at the Institute of Technology, Sligo, and KLC School of Design in London. Thank you also to my clients, especially Jane and Miles from Shells Surf Café, for allowing me to include their spaces in this book.

Thanks also to the Leitrim Integrated Development Company and Michael Comiskey, who were instrumental in the 2013 'Love Letter to the West' project being realised. To the many journalists, newspapers and magazines that have included my work in the press over the last few years, I am truly grateful. Thank you Leslie Ann Horgan and my newspaper editor Conor O'Donnell for giving me the chance to get my garden stories out there.

Many of the images are from my own gallery, but this book would not be what it is without the beautiful work of the talented photographers featured. Thank you to Colin Gillen – the photo rock star – and the talented Suzy McCanny for her wonderful images. Thanks also go out to Dara Craul, Donal Murphy and Sean and Yvette photography.

In no particular order, I would like to thank these people for their encouragement and invaluable advice on writing. The amazingly talented Kate Winter, who is a true inspiration. Love you girl (and your two boys too!). A special thank you to Rory Martin for encouragement across the pond and to Marilin North who helped me scheme on most creative projects to date ... and of course the book club girls. You know who you are.

Most of all thank you to my amazing family in Ireland, Rio and Germany. Especially to you Armando (and Maia of course) for putting up with my late evenings and early starts while writing this book. x

PHOTOGRAPHY AND DESIGN CREDITS

Leonie Cornelius's own photographs and associated designer credits are as follows:

Designer Credits for Bloom in the Park: **Alan Rudden:** pp. 34–35, p. 36 (top left), pp. 92–93, p. 102 (bottom left), p. 109 (bottom left and right), pp. 126–127, p. 178 (bottom); **Andrew Christopher Designs:** p. 31 (bottom), p. 100 (top), p. 101 (top), p. 162 (bottom), p. 182 (top); **Deirdre Pender:** p. 100 (bottom), p. 103 (bottom), p. 117 (bottom), p. 123 (bottom), p. 160 (top), p. 183 (left); **Niall Maxwell:** p. 99 (bottom), p. 102 (top), pp. 104–105, p. 107 (top right and bottom), pp. 200–201; **Fiann Ó Nualláin:** p. 186 (top), 187 (top right); **Jane McCorkell:** p. 103 (top), p. 109 (top), pp. 170–171, p. 184 (top); **Alexandra Hollingsworth:** p. 91 (top); **Sofi Dosa:** p. 108 (bottom), pp. 166–167; **Brian Burke:** p. 14 (top); **Alan Coffey:** p. 189 (top); **Cian Hawes:** p. 101 (bottom), p. 122 (bottom), pp. 192–193, p. 207 (top); **Barry Kavanagh:** p. 14 (bottom), p. 122 (top), p. 206 (bottom left); **Marion Keogh:** p. 168 (bottom left), **James Purdy:** p. 178 (top); **UCD, Dr Caroline Elliott-Kingston & Nicola Haines:** p. 187 (left); **Breffni McGeough:** p. 36 (bottom), p. 191 (top); **Paul Foley:** p. 179 (bottom).

Chaumont sur Loire garden festival, France: p. 29 (top right), p. 72 (top left), p. 179 (top left), p. 182 (bottom), p. 183 (bottom right), p. 185; p. 188 (top); **Annette Coleman:** p. 36 (top right), p. 77 (bottom), pp. 82–83 (all); p. 183 (top right), p. 206 (top and bottom right); **Neven Maguire's restaurant garden:** p. 76, p. 77 (top); **The Organic Centre,** Leitrim: p. 79; **John Monahan of Noji architects:** p. 125; **Suzy Cahn:** p. 184 (bottom), p. 189 (bottom left); **Wendy Kochmann:** p. 187 (bottom right); **Leonie Cornelius for Shells Surf Café:** pp. 110–111, pp. 118–119, pp. 138–139, p. 142 (middle), pp. 194–195, case study pp. 214–217 (all).

The author and publisher would like to thank the following photographers, designers and architects for the permission to use their wonderful photographs in this book:

Colin Gillen: front cover, pp. 2–3, p. 6, p. 32 (right), p. 33 (top), p. 120, p. 121 (all), pp. 148–149, pp. 168–169 (centre), p. 176, p. 204 (top), p. 205, p. 207 (bottom), pp. 208–209, case study pp. 218–221 (all), p. 223.

Suzy McCanny photography: back cover, pp. 8–9, p. 15 (bottom), p. 21, pp. 128–129 (all), pp. 136–137, pp. 154–155, pp. 156–157, pp. 158–159, p. 162 (top), pp. 174–175, pp. 202–203, case study pp. 210–213 (all).

James Basson-Scapedesign: pp. 10–11, p. 13 (bottom), pp. 16–17, p. 20 (left), p. 31 (top), p. 33 (bottom), 38 (all), p. 50 (top), p. 86 (top), pp. 172–173.

Dara Craul for **June Blake:** pp. 4–5, p. 12 (top) p. 13 (top), pp. 18–19, p. 32 (bottom left), p. 197.

Donal Murphy Photography for **Kingston Lafferty Designs:** pp. 26–27, p. 28, p. 29 (top left and bottom), p. 108 (top), p. 198 (top).

Sean and Yvette Photography for NOJI-John Monahan Architects: p. 39, p. 124, pp. 180–181.

Marilin North: p. 130 (bottom), p. 132 (bottom).

All other images: **shutterstock.com**